Qualifications and Credit Framework (QCF)

AQ2013

LEVEL 2 CERTIFICATE IN ACCOUNTING

WORKBOOK

Computerised Accounting

2014 Edition

For assessments from September 2014

Second edition June 2014
ISBN 9781 4727 0946 2

Previous edition
ISBN 9781 4727 0360 6

British Library Cataloguing-in-Publication Data
A catalogue record for this book is available from the British
Library

Published by
BPP Learning Media Ltd
BPP House
Aldine Place
London
W12 8AA

www.bpp.com/learningmedia

Printed in the United Kingdom by Martins of Berwick
Sea View Works
Spittal
Berwick-Upon-Tweed
TD15 1RS

CONTENTS

Introduction

Chapters and chapter tasks

A NOTE ABOUT COPYRIGHT

Dear Customer

What does the little © mean and why does it matter?

Your market-leading BPP books, course materials and e-learning materials do not write and update themselves. People write them on their own behalf or as employees of an organisation that invests in this activity. Copyright law protects their livelihoods. It does so by creating rights over the use of the content.

Breach of copyright is a form of theft – as well being a criminal offence in some jurisdictions, it is potentially a serious breach of professional ethics.

With current technology, things might seem a bit hazy but, basically, without the express permission of BPP Learning Media:

- Photocopying our materials is a breach of copyright

- Scanning, ripcasting or conversion of our digital materials into different file formats, uploading them to facebook or emailing them to your friends is a breach of copyright

You can, of course, sell your books, in the form in which you have bought them – once you have finished with them. (Is this fair to your fellow students? We update for a reason). Please note the e-products are sold on a single user licence basis: we do not supply 'unlock' codes to people who have bought them secondhand.

And what about outside the UK? BPP Learning Media strives to make our materials available at prices students can afford by local printing arrangements, pricing policies and partnerships which are clearly listed on our website. A tiny minority ignore this and indulge in criminal activity by illegally photocopying our material or supporting organisations that do. If they act illegally and unethically in one area, can you really trust them?

BPP LEARNING MEDIA'S AAT MATERIALS

The AAT's assessments fall within the **Qualifications and Credit Framework** and most papers are assessed by way of an on demand **computer based assessment**. BPP Learning Media has invested heavily to ensure our materials are as relevant as possible for this method of assessment. In particular, our **suite of online resources** ensures that you are prepared for online testing by allowing you to practise numerous online tasks that are similar to the tasks you will encounter in the AAT's assessments.

Resources

The BPP range of resources comprises:

- **Texts**, covering all the knowledge and understanding needed by students, with numerous illustrations of 'how it works', practical examples and tasks for you to use to consolidate your learning. The majority of tasks within the texts have been written in an interactive style that reflects the style of the online tasks we anticipate the AAT will set. When you purchase a Text you are also granted free access to your Text content online.

- **Question Banks**, including additional learning questions plus the AAT's sample assessment(s) and a number of BPP full practice assessments. Full answers to all questions and assessments, prepared by BPP Learning Media Ltd, are included. Our question banks are provided free of charge in an online environment containing tasks similar to those you will encounter in the AAT's testing environment. This means you can become familiar with being tested in an online environment prior to completing the real assessment.

- **Passcards**, which are handy pocket-sized revision tools designed to fit in a handbag or briefcase to enable you to revise anywhere at anytime. All major points are covered in the Passcards which have been designed to assist you in consolidating knowledge.

- **Workbooks**, which have been designed to cover the units that are assessed by way of computer based project/case study. The workbooks contain many practical tasks to assist in the learning process and also a sample assessment or project to work through.

- **Lecturers' resources**, for units assessed by computer based assessments. These provide a further bank of tasks, answers and full practice assessments for classroom use, available separately only to lecturers whose colleges adopt BPP Learning Media material.

This Workbook for Computerised Accounting has been written specifically to ensure comprehensive yet concise coverage of the AAT's **AQ2013** learning outcomes and assessment criteria.

The format of the Computerised Accounting assessment is subject to revision and tutors and students should ensure they check the latest AAT guidance for Computerised Accounting before preparing for the assessment.

Each chapter contains:

- Clear, step-by-step explanation of the topic

- Logical progression and linking from one chapter to the next

- Numerous hands-on exercises and illustrations

- Interactive tasks within the chapter itself, with answers following the chapters

- Test your learning questions, again with answers supplied following the chapters

The emphasis in all tasks and questions is on the practical application of the skills acquired. At the end of the workbook is the AAT sample assessment plus an additional BPP practice assessment.

Supplements

From time to time we may need to publish supplementary materials to one of our titles. This can be for a variety of reasons, from a small change in the AAT unit guidance to new legislation coming into effect between editions.

You should check our supplements page regularly for anything that may affect your learning materials. All supplements are available free of charge on our supplements page on our website at:

http://www.bpp.com/about-bpp/aboutBPP/StudentInfo#q4

Customer feedback

If you have any comments about this book, please email ianblackmore@bpp.com or write to Ian Blackmore, AAT Range Manager, BPP Learning Media Ltd, BPP House, Aldine Place, London W12 8AA.

Any feedback we receive is taken into consideration when we periodically update our materials, including comments on style, depth and coverage of AAT standards.

In addition, although our products pass through strict technical checking and quality control processes, unfortunately errors may occasionally slip through when producing material to tight deadlines.

When we learn of an error in a batch of our printed materials, either from internal review processes or from customers using our materials, we want to make sure customers are made aware of this as soon as possible and the appropriate action is taken to minimise the impact on student learning.

As a result, when we become aware of any such errors we will:

1) Include details of the error and, if necessary, PDF prints of any revised pages under the related subject heading on our 'supplements' page at: http://www.bpp.com/about-bpp/aboutBPP/StudentInfo#q4

2) Update the source files ahead of any further printing of the materials

3) Investigate the reason for the error and take appropriate action to minimise the risk of reoccurrence.

A NOTE ON TERMINOLOGY

The AAT AQ2013 standards and assessments use international terminology based on International Financial Reporting Standards (IFRSs). Although you may be familiar with UK terminology, you need to now know the equivalent international terminology for your assessments.

The following information is taken from an article on the AAT's website and compares IFRS terminology with UK GAAP terminology. It then goes on to describe the impact of IFRS terminology on students studying for each level of the AAT QCF qualification.

Note that since the article containing the information below was published, there have been changes made to some IFRSs. Therefore BPP Learning Media have updated the table and other information below to reflect these changes.

In particular, the primary performance statement under IFRSs which was formerly known as the 'income statement' or the 'statement of comprehensive income' is now called the 'statement of profit or loss' or the 'statement of profit or loss and other comprehensive income'.

What is the impact of IFRS terms on AAT assessments?

The list shown in the table that follows gives the 'translation' between UK GAAP and IFRS.

UK GAAP	IFRS
Final accounts	Financial statements
Trading and profit and loss account	**Statement of profit or loss (or statement of profit or loss and other comprehensive income)**
Turnover or Sales	Revenue or Sales Revenue
Sundry income	Other operating income
Interest payable	Finance costs
Sundry expenses	Other operating costs
Operating profit	Profit from operations
Net profit/loss	Profit/Loss for the year/period
Balance sheet	**Statement of financial position**
Fixed assets	Non-current assets
Net book value	Carrying amount
Tangible assets	Property, plant and equipment

UK GAAP	IFRS
Reducing balance depreciation	Diminishing balance depreciation
Depreciation/Depreciation expense(s)	Depreciation charge(s)
Stocks	Inventories
Trade debtors or Debtors	Trade receivables
Prepayments	Other receivables
Debtors and prepayments	Trade and other receivables
Cash at bank and in hand	Cash and cash equivalents
Trade creditors or Creditors	Trade payables
Accruals	Other payables
Creditors and accruals	Trade and other payables
Long-term liabilities	Non-current liabilities
Capital and reserves	Equity (limited companies)
Profit and loss balance	Retained earnings
Minority interest	Non-controlling interest
Cash flow statement	**Statement of cash flows**

This is certainly not a comprehensive list, which would run to several pages, but it does cover the main terms that you will come across in your studies and assessments. However, you won't need to know all of these in the early stages of your studies – some of the terms will not be used until you reach Level 4. For each level of the AAT qualification, the points to bear in mind are as follows:

Level 2 Certificate in Accounting

The IFRS terms do not impact greatly at this level. Make sure you are familiar with 'receivables' (also referred to as 'trade receivables'), 'payables' (also referred to as 'trade payables'), and 'inventories'. The terms sales ledger and purchases ledger – together with their control accounts – will continue to be used. Sometimes the control accounts might be called 'trade receivables control account' and 'trade payables control account'. The other term to be aware of is 'non-current asset' – this may be used in some assessments.

Level 3 Diploma in Accounting

At this level you need to be familiar with the term 'financial statements'. The financial statements comprise a 'statement of profit or loss' (previously known as an income statement), and a 'statement of financial position'. In the statement of profit or loss the term 'revenue' or 'sales revenue' takes the place of 'sales', and 'profit for the year' replaces 'net profit'. Other terms may be used in the statement of financial position – eg 'non-current assets' and 'carrying amount'. However, specialist limited company terms are not required at this level.

Level 4 Diploma in Accounting

At Level 4 a wider range of IFRS terms is needed, and in the case of Financial statements, are already in use – particularly those relating to limited companies. Note especially that a statement of profit or loss becomes a 'statement of profit or loss and other comprehensive income'.

Note: The information above was taken from an AAT article from the 'assessment news' area of the AAT website (www.aat.org.uk). However, it has been adapted by BPP Learning Media for changes in international terminology since the article was published and for any changes needed to reflect the move from AQ2010 to AQ2013.

ASSESSMENT STRATEGY

Computerised Accounting (CPAG) is assessed at Level 2. The unit may be assessed either using workplace evidence or by completing the computer-based project set centrally by the AAT. The following information is based on the assessment strategy section of the AAT's guidance document for this unit in issue at the time of writing this Workbook.

Computer based project

The time allowed to complete the Computerised Accounting assessment is 2 hours.

The assessment will be based on a business organisation and comprise a series of tasks that ask the student to input data into a computerised accounting system and produce reports, allowing the student to demonstrate the skills and knowledge necessary to use computerised accounting software at Level 2.

The assessment has not been designed for use with any one particular accounting software package. The AAT recognise that a variety of accounting software packages are available and can be used, but the one chosen must be capable of performing the procedures outlined in this document.

The candidate will be asked to print documents and reports that will provide the information needed for marking purposes. If the training provider's computerised accounting system allows for the generation of PDFs, these can be generated instead of hard copy prints. Screenshots saved as image files are also acceptable.

The assessment tasks, along with the related assessment criteria and topics are shown below.

Task	Learning outcome	Assessment criteria	Task topic
1	1	1.2	Set up customer records
2	1	1.3	Set up supplier records
3	1	1.1	Set up nominal ledger accounts
4	2	2.1	Process invoices and credit notes for customers
5	3	3.1	Process invoices and credit notes for suppliers
6	2 (6)	2.2 (6.1)	Allocate monies received
7	3 (6)	3.2 (6.1)	Allocate monies paid
8	4	4.1	Process receipts and payments for non-credit transactions.

Task	Learning outcome	Assessment criteria	Task topic
9	4	4.2	Process recurring receipts and payments (standing orders and direct debits)
10	4	4.3	Process petty cash receipts and payments.
11	5	5.1, 5.2	Process journal entries
12	4	4.4	Perform a periodic bank reconciliation
13	7	7.1, 7.2	Maintain the safety and security of computerised data
14	6	6.1, 6.2	Produce reports

The summary below describes the ability and skills students at this level must successfully demonstrate to achieve competence.

Competence at Level 2

Summary

Achievement at Level 2 reflects the ability to select and use relevant knowledge, ideas, skills and procedures to complete well-defined tasks and address straightforward problems. It includes taking responsibility for completing tasks and procedures and exercising autonomy and judgement subject to overall direction or guidance.

Knowledge and understanding

- Use understanding of facts, procedures and ideas to complete well-defined tasks and address straightforward problems.
- Interpret relevant information and ideas.
- Be aware of the types of information that are relevant to the area of study or work.

Application and action

- Complete well-defined, generally routine tasks and address straightforward problems.
- Select and use relevant skills and procedures.
- Identify, gather and use relevant information to inform actions.
- Identify how effective actions have been.

Autonomy and accountability

- Take responsibility for completing tasks and procedures.
- Exercise autonomy and judgement subject to overall direction or guidance.

Workplace evidence

With guidance and support from training providers, students can provide workplace evidence to be assessed locally by their training provider. The local assessor (training provider) will be required to ensure that all assessment criteria are covered.

AAT UNIT GUIDE

The following section reproduces the AAT's guidance for this unit at the time of writing of this Workbook.

Computerised Accounting (CPAG) delivery guidance

Introduction

Please note that this document is subject to annual review and revision to ensure that is accurately reflects the assessment criteria.

This Level 2 unit is about using a computerised accounting system to maintain records of business transactions including sales and purchases, receipts and payments, and to prepare reports.

The unit complements knowledge of manual record keeping systems gained in other Level 2 units, specifically processing bookkeeping transactions and control accounts, journals and the banking system. Prior knowledge of manual record keeping systems is an advantage, but not essential, when studying this unit.

The purpose of the unit

Computerised accounting systems are widely used in business and other organisations. They speed up the process of recording accounting transactions, automatically updating all relevant records following the input of a single transaction and enabling the instant generation of reports for management.

This practical unit covers the fundamental principles required to use a computerised accounting system and will allow MT students to develop skills that are valued in the workplace. The unit includes the skills needed to record accounting transactions with credit customers and credit suppliers as well as recording transactions involving the bank, petty cash and other nominal ledger accounts.

Those who have achieved this Level 2 unit will not only benefit employers through the relevant skills they have acquired but also through the knowledge they have gained, which will enable them to use a computerised amounting software system confidently to record a range of accounting transactions and generate up to date information for management.

Learning objectives

Students will be able to use a computerised accounting system to set up accounting records, enter accounting transactions, perform a bank reconciliation, correct errors and produce a range of reports. They will also be able to maintain the security of accounting information using passwords and backup routines.

Guidance on delivery

General

This document should be read in conjunction with the standards for this unit, which include reference to general ledger accounts. AAT guidance and assessment material for this unit will refer to nominal ledger accounts and not general ledger accounts.

Students must be able to use a computerised accounting system to perform the procedures specified in this document. They must be able to take and print screenshots of their work. They must be able to refer to the help guidelines included in the software package, and respond to computer generated error messages, making use of these as required.

It is recognised that a variety of accounting software packages are available, and can be used, but the one chosen must be capable of performing the procedures outlined in this document.

Throughout the unit

- Students should check and, where appropriate, correct their own work

- Students should be able to process transactions involving different rates of VAT:
    - Standard rate
    - Not applicable

The rate of VAT will always be given in assessments.

For assessment purposes, the software should be set up with the system software date, company details and the date of the financial year, all of which will be given in the assessment. These details should be entered at the start of the assessment; this setup does not form part of the standards, therefore training providers may assist students with this.

LO1 – Enter accounting data at the beginning of an accounting period

1.1 Set up general ledger accounts, entering opening balances where appropriate. Students must be able to set up nominal ledger accounts, including:

- Selecting appropriate accounts from the default list of accounts provided by the software

- Amending the account names used in the default list of accounts provided by the software, for example change 'sales' to 'sales of product A'

- Adding new accounts to the default list of accounts provided by the software

- Entering the date and amount of any opening balances

- Checking opening entries by generating an initial trial balance

L01 – Enter accounting data at the beginning of an accounting period

To meet the requirements of this assessment criterion, students may, for example, be provided with a list of account names and opening balances (if applicable) and asked to enter these into the computer.

1.2 Set up customer accounts, entering opening balances where appropriate.

1.3 Set up supplier accounts, entering opening balances where appropriate.

Students must be able to set up accounts for credit customers and credit suppliers, including:

- Entering customer/supplier name, address, payment terms

- Entering a given customer/supplier account code

- Entering the date of the opening balance

- Entering the amount of any opening balance as a single figure only, that is, not as individual transactions

To meet the requirements of these assessment criteria, students may, for example, be provided with details of customers and suppliers and opening balances (if applicable) and asked to enter these into the computer.

L02 – Record customer transactions

L03 – Record supplier transactions

2.1 Process sales invoices and credit notes, accounting for VAT.

3.1 Process purchases invoices and credit notes, accounting for VAT.

Students must be able to poet entries to record sales and purchases invoices and sales and purchases credit notes, including:

- Selecting the appropriate customer or supplier account code

- Selecting appropriate nominal ledger account codes, including codes for nominal ledger accounts not previously set up

- Entering the date, details and amount of the transaction

- Selecting the appropriate code to account for VAT

Purchases invoices and credit notes can relate to the purchase of materials/goods for resale and of expenses.

To meet the requirements of these assessment criteria, students may, for example, be given source documents (invoices and credit notes) or a listing of sales/purchases and sales/purchases returns and asked to make entries into the computer to record the relevant transactions. If appropriate students may choose to enter transactions singly or in batches, the assessment will not specify the method to be used.

L02 – Record customer transactions

L03 – Record supplier transactions

2.2 Allocate monies received from customers in partial or full payment of invoices and balances.

3.2 Allocate monies paid to suppliers in full or partial settlement of invoices and balances.

Students must be able to post payments received from credit customers and payments made to credit suppliers as follows:

- Payments which are in full settlement of invoices and/or opening balances

- Payments which are in full settlement of invoices and/or opening balances but include credit notes

- Payments on account

This includes:

- Selecting the appropriate customer or supplier account code
- Entering the date, details and amount of the receipt or payment
- Allocating payments against opening balances, invoices and credit notes
- Posting payments as a payment on account
- Producing remittance advice notes for payments to suppliers (see LO6)

Payments in this instance can comprise cash, cheques, and automated payments.

Set off payments (contra entries) and settlement discounts will NOT be tested.

To meet the requirements of these assessment criteria, students may, for example, be given a listing of receipts and/or payments or source documents (for example, remittance advice notes from customers) and asked to make entries into the computer to record the relevant transactions.

L04 – Record and reconcile bank and cash transactions

4.1 Process receipts and payments for non-credit transactions

Students must be able to post entries to record transactions, which include VAT where appropriate, as follows:

- Cash purchases and sales

- Sundry income received , for example, commission received

- Payments for items other than the purchase of goods, eg the purchase of a non-current asset, the payment of rent

L04 – Record and reconcile bank and cash transactions

- Transfers between bank accounts, for example, current account to deposit account

- Other receipts and payments, for example, drawings by the owner, receipt of a bank loan

This includes:

- Selecting the appropriate bank and nominal ledger account codes
- Entering the date, details and amount of the receipt or payment
- Selecting the appropriate code to account for VAT

Receipts and payments in this instance can comprise cash, cheques, debit card and automated payments. Credit card receipts and payments will NOT be tested.

To meet the requirements of this assessment criterion, students may, for example, be given source documents, such as cash receipts, and/or information via email or other internal document and asked to make entries into the computer to record the relevant transactions.

4.2 Process recurring receipts and payments

Students must be able to set up and process recurring bank receipts and payments, including:

- Identifying the appropriate transaction type

- Selecting the appropriate bank and nominal ledger account codes

- Entering the frequency, duration and posting dates of the receipt or payment

- Entering the details and amount of the receipt or payment

- Selecting the appropriate code to account for VAT

- Processing the first receipt or payment

Students will NOT be expected to set up or process the following transactions:

- Recurring receipts from customers or payments to suppliers
- Recurring journal entries
- Recurring transactions between bank accounts.
- Perpetual transactions, that is transactions with no finish date

To meet the requirements of this assessment criterion, students may, for example, be given a standing order/direct debit listing or information via email or other internal document and asked to make entries into the computer to record the relevant transactions.

Students will be asked to take a screen shot showing the set-up of the recurring entry.

L04 – Record and reconcile bank and cash transactions

4.3 Process petty cash receipts and payments, accounting for VAT

Students must be able to post entries to record petty cash payments, which may include VAT where appropriate. They must also be able to record amounts received to reimburse, or increase, the petty cash float.

This includes:

- Selecting the appropriate petty cash, bank and nominal ledger account codes

- Entering the date, details and amount of the receipt or payment

- Selecting the appropriate code to account for VAT

Students will NOT be expected to understand the Imprest system or calculate the amount required to reimburse the petty cash float.

To meet the requirements of this assessment criterion, students may be given petty cash vouchers and asked to make entries into the computer to record petty cash payments. Students may also be given a completed petty cash reimbursement request or information via email or other internal document and asked to make entries into the computer to record petty cash receipts.

4.4 Perform a periodic bank reconciliation

Students must be able to post entries to record transactions shown on a bank statement, for example, bank charges that have not previously been recorded. Students will NOT be expected to identify such transactions, merely to record them.

This includes:

- Selecting the appropriate bank and nominal ledger account codes
- Entering the date, details and amount of the receipt or payment
- Selecting the appropriate code to account for VAT

Students must be able to complete the appropriate steps, according to the computerised accounting package in use, to reconcile the nominal ledger bank balance with the balance on a bank statement. If appropriate, students should be able to trace and correct their own errors.

To meet the requirements of this assessment criterion, students may, for example, be given a bank statement and asked to make entries into the computer to update the bank account and then perform a bank reconciliation. The opening balance on the bank statement will always be equal to the opening balance in the bank account in the nominal ledger.

L05 – Be able to use journals to enter accounting transactions

5.1 Process journals for accounting transactions

5.2 Use the journal to correct errors

Students must be able to post entries to record given journal transactions, including:

- Selecting the appropriate nominal ledger account codes
- Entering the date, details and amount of the transactions
- Selecting the appropriate code to account for VAT

Given journal entries can include any of the accounting transactions previously detailed in this document and journals to correct errors. Students should also be able to post journal entries to correct their own errors that may occur during the assessment.

To meet the requirements of these assessment criteria, students will be given journal entries and asked to make entries into the computer to record the relevant transactions. Journal entries to correct errors may, for example, include errors in opening balances and errors in transactions input in earlier tasks.

L06 – Produce reports

6.1 Produce these routine reports for customers and suppliers:

- Day books
- Account activity
- Aged analysis
- Statements or remittance advice notes

6.2 Produce these routine reports from the general ledger

- Trial balance
- Audit trail
- Account activity

Students must be able to produce the following reports:

- Sales, purchases, sales returns and purchases returns day books

- All sales ledger (customer) accounts, or specific sales ledger (customer) accounts only

- All purchases ledger (supplier) accounts, or specific purchases ledger (supplier) accounts only aged trade receivables and aged trade payables analysis

- Statements of account to be sent to credit customers

- Remittance advice notes to be sent with a payment to credit suppliers

L06 – Produce reports

- Trial balance

- Audit trail showing full details of all transactions, including details of receipts/payments

- Allocated to items in customer/supplier accounts and details of items in the bank account that have been reconciled

- All nominal ledger accounts, or specific nominal ledger accounts only

To meet the requirements of these assessment criteria, students will be asked to print some or all of the reports specified above. For assessment purposes note the alternatives to 'print' specified in this document.

L07 – Maintain the safety and security of data held in the computerised accounting system

7.1 Make a copy of accounting data using the backup function of the accounting software

Students must be able to use the back-up facility within the computerised accounting system in use to back up computerised data to a suitable storage medium.

Students should be able to back up their data at regular intervals throughout the assessment, not just when instructed to do so.

To meet the requirements of this assessment criterion, students will be asked to back up data to a suitable storage medium, for example at the end of the assessment. Students will be asked to print a screen shot of the backup screen showing the file name and location of the backup copy

7.2 Use a software password to protect accounting information

Students must be able to enter a given password into the computerised accounting system to restrict access to computerised data.

To meet the requirements of this assessment criterion, students will be asked to print a screenshot of the screen which shows where a password would be entered.

SAGE SOFTWARE

Do students have to use Sage to complete this unit?

No. Students **do not** have to use Sage in their AAT Computerised Accounting Software assessment.

The AAT recognise that a variety of accounting software packages are available and can be used. The only stipulation the AAT make is that the package used must be capable of performing the procedures outlined in the learning outcomes and assessment criteria.

Do students need access to Sage software to use this Workbook?

Students that don't have Sage software may still pick up some useful information from this book, for example the practice assessments.

However, those students with access to Sage will find it easier to work through the practical exercises than users of other accounting software packages.

Refer to the next page for details of how Sage software may be bought, for educational purposes, at very reasonable prices.

Why does this Workbook refer to Sage Instant?

To explain and demonstrate the skills required in this unit, it is necessary to provide practical examples and exercises. This requires the use of computerised accounting software.

This Workbook provides examples taken from Sage Instant Accounts.

What version do I need?

The illustrations in this Workbook are taken from Sage Instant Accounts 2013.

Sage upgrade their software regularly. However, many features and functions remain the same from version to version. For this reason, it is expected that this Workbook will remain valid for a number of future versions of Sage.

Some training centres may use different Sage packages or different versions of Sage. Although the screens and menus may appear slightly different you should still be able to perform the tasks contained in this Workbook.

How do I buy Sage software?

Colleges

If this book is used by students in a college environment, the college will need Sage installed on student computers. This publication is based on Sage Instant Accounts 2013 but colleges may use a different version of Sage or a different Sage product such as Sage Accounts 50. Sage Instant and Sage 50 packages are very similar in their operation with Sage 50 Accounts being aimed at larger businesses.

Colleges wanting to purchase Sage products should **contact Sage** in the UK. Contact details can be found at www.sage.co.uk.

Individual students

Individual students are able to buy **Sage Instant Accounts** from BPP Learning Media for a very reasonable price. This must be for educational purposes. For details you should contact BPP Learning Media customer services on 0845 075 1100 or email learningmedia@bpp.com

Are Sage data files provided with this book?

No. Sage data files aren't provided because the material is written in such a way that they aren't required.

New installations of Sage allow users to access a blank ledger suitable for experimenting. Instructions are provided in this book that enable a new blank ledger to be created.

chapter 1:
SAGE – PART 1

chapter coverage 📖

You will be required to prove your competence in the use of computerised accounting software by completing an assessment. Assessments are likely to include a series of exercises, for example entering customer and supplier details, posting transactions such as journals, invoices and credit notes, and obtaining reports and print-outs.

This chapter explains how you might complete the hands-on computerised accounts parts of an assessment. It is by no means a comprehensive guide to computerised accounting.

The illustrations in this chapter and the next chapter are from Sage Instant Accounts, which is just one of many packages that you might use. We use a Sage package because these are popular amongst small/medium-sized businesses in the UK, and with colleges for training purposes.

There are a large number of illustrations in this chapter, so don't be put off if it seems long – it should be relatively quick and easy to work through.

The topics covered in this chapter are:

- ✍ Accounting packages
- ✍ Assessments
- ✍ Company data and the general (nominal) ledger
- ✍ Customer and supplier data
- ✍ Journals
- ✍ Entering invoices
- ✍ Password protection
- ✍ Help!

ACCOUNTING PACKAGES

Accounting packages range from simple 'off the shelf' analysed cash book style packages to heavy-duty Enterprise Resource Management systems used in large organisations. Very large organisations often have a system that has been built specifically for them, made up of components from a variety of software suppliers, or written for them on a one-off basis.

Obviously, we cannot even begin to cover the vast range of available packages, but we can illustrate the features of a typical package, and the most popular one in the UK among small- to medium-sized businesses is Sage.

Sage produces a variety of accounting packages and this book deals with Sage Instant Accounts. The illustrations in this chapter are taken from Sage Instant Accounts 2013. In the remainder of this chapter we will just use the word 'Sage' to refer to Sage Instant Accounts.

Hands-on

The illustrations in this Workbook are taken from Sage.

Sage upgrade their software regularly. However, many features and functions remain the same from version to version. Some training centres may use different Sage packages or different versions of Sage. The different Sage packages for small and medium sized businesses are based on common principles and are very similar in their operation when it comes to performing the tasks included in this Workbook. Some screens and menus may appear slightly different depending on the age or version of the product you are using, but you should be able to work your way through the tasks.

If possible we strongly recommend that you sit at a computer equipped with a version of Sage as you read through this chapter. Most of the activities assume that you are doing this and can complete the tasks we describe as you go along.

Finding your way about: terminology

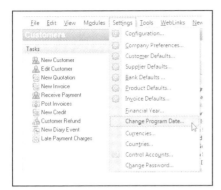

We'll assume that you know what we mean when we say 'menu' and 'button', but there may be some other terms that you are not sure of, so here is a quick guide. In this chapter we will use bold text when referring to something that you will see on screen, such as a button or a menu or a label beside or above a box. For example we might say 'click on the **Settings** menu and choose **Change Program Date**'.

Whilst you can use the buttons on the toolbars as your main starting point it is useful to familiarise yourself with the Settings and Modules buttons as the content of these rarely change although the layout and position of the buttons can vary between different versions. Here is the main toolbar that you can see at the bottom left of the screen when you open up Sage Version 12 or later, with the **Customers** button highlighted.

When the **Customers** button is highlighted, the following toolbar appears at the top of the screen.

Also, a list of customer-related tasks appears at the top left. Some of the top line of buttons and some of those on the left duplicate actions.

Most of what you do involves you making entries in **'fields'** – for example the **A/C** field and the **Date** field in the next illustration.

Sometimes you need to select a 'tab' to view the part of the program we refer to. For instance in this example the **Activity** tab is selected.

Finally, make sure that you know where the **Tab** key is on your keyboard (usually above the Caps Lock key) and also that you are aware of the function keys (**F1**, **F2** and so on, usually along the top). The **Esc** key is also very useful for closing windows quickly.

Defaults

Computerised packages make extensive use of 'defaults', which are the most common entries. When you start entering data you will often find that Sage has done some of the work already, using the default options that would normally be chosen. This saves a great deal of time, but you should always glance at the default entries in case they are not the ones you want. This will become clearer as you start using the package.

Screen captures and screen prints

During the assessment, for certain tasks, you will be asked print a screenshot of the screen to provide evidence that you have completed the task correctly.

To take a screen capture of an entire screen, on your keyboard press **Print Screen** or **PrtScn**. To capture the active window only press **Alt + Print Screen** or **ALT + PrtScn** (on some keyboards the key may be labelled PrtSc).

These actions capture the screen or window onto the computer's clipboard. The image can then be pasted into another application (using **CTRL + V**) such as *Word* from where the image can be printed. **Please ensure you are able to complete this action as it is an assessment requirement.**

ASSESSMENTS

Your AAT assessment will involve a number of practical tasks that test your competence in the assessment criteria.

Before you start...

Before you start, you should find out from your assessor what the arrangements are for:

- Opening the accounting package and logging in, if necessary
- Changing any overall company details or settings, if required
- Creating new accounts as necessary
- Posting transactions and completing other assessment tasks
- Making your own back-ups
- Printing out or exporting your work

Backing-up and restoring

Making backups in essential when working on computers in general and, of course, this also applies to the data in your accounting system.

Unlike a program such as a word processor or a spreadsheet, when you make an entry in Sage, that data is saved immediately. This means that you can post an invoice, say, then close down the program. Your invoice will not be lost: it will still be there when you next open the program.

In Sage a back-up is created by clicking on the **File** menu (top left of screen) and choosing **Backup**. Fairly logical. You'll be asked if you want the program to check your data first, and it is worth doing this occasionally.

Then you will need to choose a name for your back-up file and a location.

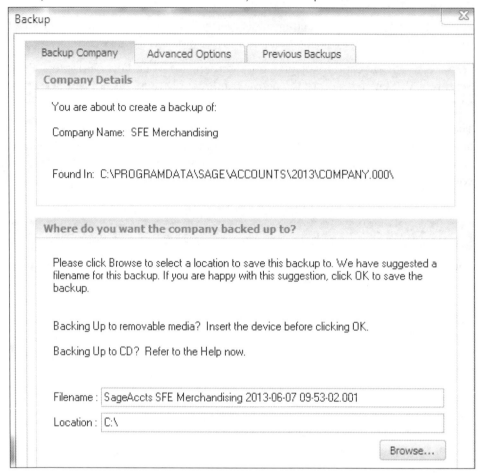

The program suggests a name based on the current date and a number but you can edit the name. During the assessment you may be instructed to make a backup and **you will be told which file name to use**. You should make sure you use the name given when completing an assessment task asking you to make a back up.

Note that you should also back up your data at regular intervals and not just when instructed to do so by an assessment task. This will help to avoid any unnecessary loss of data.

In the preceding example shown in the screen shot, the back-up will be saved in a folder on the hard drive of your computer. However, you should ask your assessor about the location you should use. Make a note of the location, such as the drive and folder used, so that you will be able to locate the data again quickly.

The **Advanced Options** allow you to choose what to back-up.

Different organisations will have different policies as to what needs to be backed up. Some may require modified Report Files to be included, some may require the Audit Trail History to be included. As a minimum, Data Files must be backed-up.

| Backup | ⊠ |

| Backup Company | Advanced Options | Previous Backups |

File types to include in backup

Type	Included?
Data Files	✓
Report Files	☐
Layout Templates	☐
TMail Database	☐
	☐
	☐
	☐
	☐

☐ Select all file types to include in backup

Restoring data is just as easy: click on **File** and then **Restore** and locate your back-up file.

When you restore from a back-up this will overwrite any data that is currently held in the program's data files, **so take care with this**. If you post a transaction and then restore an old back-up, that transaction will be lost.

You may be asked to restore a back-up before you start an assessment, because this is an excellent way of making sure that everyone starts from the same point, with the same opening balances, the same general (nominal) ledger structure and codes, and so on.

Example

The following example is based on a past sample simulation issued by the AAT (simulations were used before assessments).

Situation

SFE Merchandising is a new business that has been set up by Charlize Veron, one of Southfield Electrical's former marketing staff. Charlize is an expert on store layout and management of inventories (stocks) and she intends to sell her skills and knowledge, on a consultancy basis, to medium and large retailers to help them to optimise their sales.

Charlize has started her new venture as a sole trader and has taken on some of the risk herself. However, SFE Merchandising is part-financed by Southfield Electrical, and may well be acquired by them if this new venture is a success. Initial enquiries have been so promising that Charlize has already voluntarily registered for VAT and intends to run the standard VAT accounting scheme. (Assume the standard VAT rate is 20%).

The business commenced trading on 1 January 2013.

Tasks to be completed

It is now 31 January 2013 and you are to complete the following tasks ...

There will be 14 tasks in the real assessment involving setting up data, entering journals, posting sales and purchase transactions, obtaining print outs and so on.

You will be provided with a series of documents such as invoices, cheques, etc. We'll show you how to deal with all of this in the remainder of this Workbook.

You should now have Sage open on your computer and follow through the activities.

Task 1

Preliminary

This exercise starts with a new installation of Sage or a 'clean' company which contains no transactions.

Your college will tell you how to install Sage afresh or from where to restore the clean company.

If you are studying at home and are installing Sage for the first time on a particular PC, follow the on-screen installation instructions for a standard installation – then **go to the New Set Up instructions on the next page**.

If you are studying at home and **have an existing Sage ledger**, you may **create a new installation and a blank ledger** by following the steps below.

- **Make a backup of the existing data if you will require it again in the future**.

- Click on the File button along the top menu and select Maintenance.

- Click on the Rebuild option and untick all of the options on the left hand side. In some cases you may need to keep the nominal ledger accounts ticked to maintain the Chart of Accounts. This will vary from version to version.

- Once the rebuild is complete you will be asked to enter the month and year of the company being worked on. This is given in the scenario. If no year is given use the current year.

- Now go to the settings options and overtype the name of the existing company with that of the new company and change the program date if required to do so.

Two important points to note:

- **You will not be required to set up a new company in your real assessment. We cover this here to enable us to create the same starting point in Sage for all students.**

- **If installing the program for the first time you will need to know its Serial Number and Activation Key.**

New Set Up

The first time you open the package you are presented with a company set-up wizard.

Select the type of data you want to use

Welcome to Sage Instant Accounts

Choose one of the following options:

⊙ **Set up your Company Data**
Start using your own company's data.

○ **Open Practice Data**
Practice using the program's features without affecting your company's data. This will start as a blank set of company information.

○ **Open Demonstration Data**
See an example company we have created for you. This includes customer and supplier invoices and payments.

Select the top option to set up your company data and click **OK**.

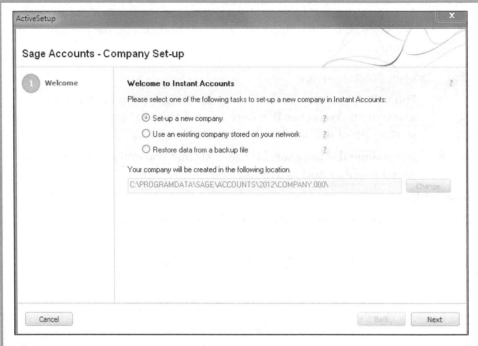

Select **Set-up a new company** and press **Next**.

If your Sage installation does not start at the set-up wizard, you can enter the company information by accessing **Settings** > **Company Preferences** from the menu at the top of the screen.

Important note: Sage generally refers to a business as a 'company' in its menus (eg Company Preferences). However this is just the terminology used by Sage, and Sage can be used for sole traders and partnerships as well as limited companies. Where menus and references in this book refer to 'company' take this as meaning 'business' unless otherwise stated. Therefore such references can encompass sole trader businesses as well as companies.

BPP
LEARNING MEDIA

COMPANY DATA AND THE GENERAL (NOMINAL) LEDGER

Company data

The name and address of the business should then be entered. This information will appear on any documents you produce with the package, such as reports and invoices, so make sure it is accurate and spelled correctly.

Enter all the information given in the screen below. Use the **Tab** key on your keyboard to move between different lines. Alternatively, click on each line, but this will slow you down, so get into the habit of using the **Tab** key to move from field to field (almost all packages work this way). When you have finished press **Next** (each time you complete a new screen you will need to press **Next** to continue – you can also use the **Back** button if you need to re-visit a screen).

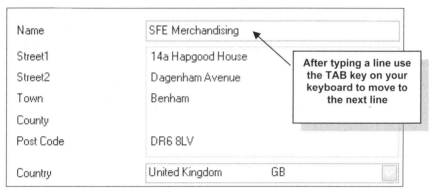

Accounts in the general (nominal) ledger

The **general ledger** is the ledger that contains all of the business's statement of profit or loss (income statement) and statement of financial position accounts. This is also known as the **nominal ledger** and 'nominal ledger' is the term used by Sage.

When a new business is first set up there is a choice between a number of different templates or 'Chart of Accounts' (COA).

The charts provided are tailored towards the type of business. In Sage Instant Accounts 2013 it gives you a choice between a Sole Trader, Partnership and Limited Company. SFE Merchandising is a sole trader so you should select this option – **Sole Trader**.

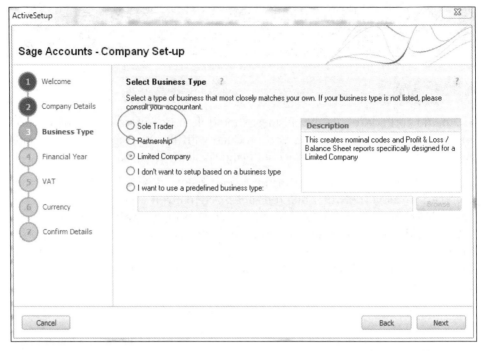

If you are using previous versions of Sage Instant Accounts or you are using Sage Accounts 50 you may be faced with a number of chart of accounts for different types of company, similar to that shown below.

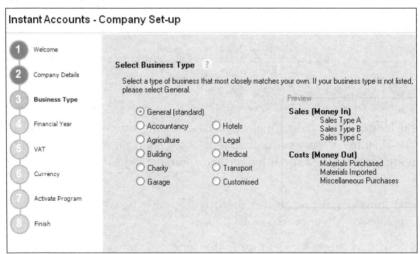

These have accounts tailored for the particular business type.

For example, the 'Hotels, Restaurants and Guest Houses' chart includes sales accounts for 'Restaurant Meals', 'Alcoholic Beverage Sales' and so on.

Many organisations use the 'General' chart, and modify it to suit their needs. If you are faced with the screen above, choose the **General (Standard)** chart of accounts.

Note that you are not confined to using the accounts that you are given by the program when you first set up the company. Certain accounts must always remain because the program will not be able to operate without them – so you will not be able to delete the main bank account, the receivables (debtors) and payables (creditors) control accounts, VAT accounts, and certain other essential accounts. But you can delete any non-essential accounts (so long as you have not yet posted any transactions to them), and you can rename them and add new accounts as required.

Financial year

Set the start of the financial year to January 2013. This can be done either by progressing through the wizard or by accessing **Settings > Financial Year** from the menu.

VAT

The business **is** VAT registered (so select **Yes** in the wizard) and is not registered for cash accounting. Using either the wizard or by choosing **Settings > Company Preferences > VAT** Enter 524 3764 51 as the VAT number.

Enter the standard VAT rate % as 20.00.

Currency

Select **Pound Sterling**, either from the wizard or **Settings > Currency** from the menu.

Activate program

If necessary, activate the program by entering the serial number and activation code supplied with the program or by your college and then click **Finish**.

On clicking Finish you may need to call Sage to fully register your product. The number to call will appear on your screen. Sage should talk you through how to register and how to restart the program having done so.

You are now ready to proceed entering the company's transactions.

New accounts and your assessment

In your assessment you may need to add new nominal ledger accounts to complete your tasks, or you may not. As you work through your assessment, before starting each task check that the accounts you will need are set up. We recommend you create any new accounts required before starting the task the account is needed in.

If the assessment includes a purchase invoice for stationery, for instance, check that there is already an 'Office stationery' overheads account before you start to post the invoice. The tasks may actually ask you to do this. For instance, you may be instructed to work through the invoices provided and write the relevant nominal ledger codes on them.

You can see which chart of accounts has been applied by choosing **Modules > Nominal Ledger** from the menu bar at the top of the screen, or by choosing **Company** from the set of buttons at the bottom left of the screen, then **Nominal Ledger** from the **Links** buttons as shown in the following illustration.

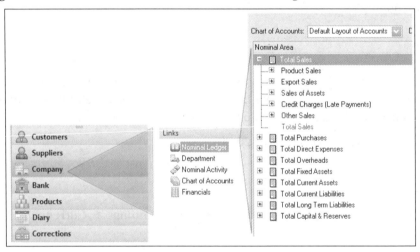

If the chart includes a long list of accounts, you can change it to the format shown above by accessing the **Layout** options at the top right of the screen and choosing **Analyser**.

The chart of accounts, above, has been grouped by type of account. These main headings can be expanded by clicking on the '+' sign next to each heading.

Expand **Total Overheads** and then **Printing and Stationery** and you will see that there is not yet a specific account for Publicity material, so we will create one.

Task 2

Create a new account for 'publicity material'.

Click on the **New Nominal** button

and the program will take you through the Nominal Record Wizard. It is possible to set up new accounts without using the wizard, but we discourage this, because it can very easily lead to problems in the way the program handles your new nominal ledger accounts when it is producing reports and financial statements.

On pressing **Next,** the first step is to decide on the **Name** of your new account (overtype 'New nominal account') and choose what **Type** of account it is.

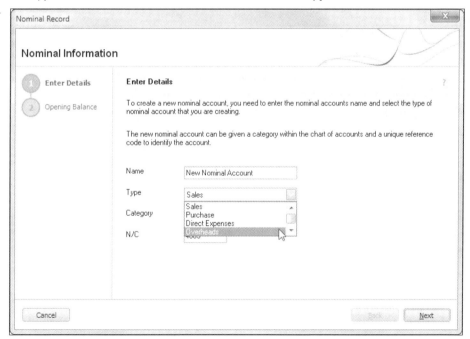

You can further refine the **Category** of account (the options available will depend on the type of account you are setting up – here Printing and Stationery) and choose an account code (**Ref**). In fact the program will suggest a code, depending on the choices you have made so far, and we strongly recommend that you accept this.

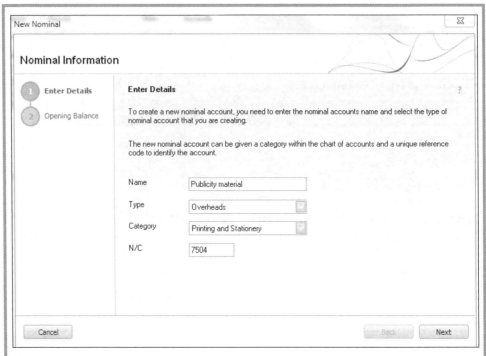

After making your selections and clicking **Next**, you will be asked if you want to **enter an opening balance**. Choose **No** and click **Create**. We cover entering opening balances later in the chapter (directly or via a journal). The options for entering opening balances are also covered in Sage Help. From the Help menu select **Contents and Index** and navigate to (or search for) **Opening Balances**.

Task 3

Vimal was in a hurry to post a transaction because he'd just had a text message and he wanted to reply. He wasn't sure what nominal account to use, so he created a new account named 'L8R'. Why might this cause problems later on?

It is also possible to change the name of existing nominal accounts. To do this you need to select the account you want to change and then click on **Nominal Record**. This brings up a screen showing details of the selected account and you can update the name field. For example you could change 'Sales Type B' to something that is more descriptive of the particular sales to be recorded in that account (eg Overseas Sales).

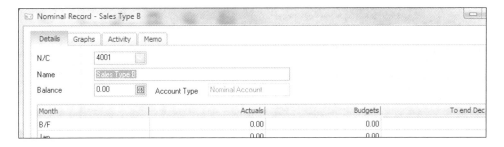

Entering opening balances in nominal ledger accounts

If you are transferring your business's accounting recording from a manual system to a computer system you will need to post opening balances to your nominal ledger.

Although you can do this using a journal (as we will see later in the chapter), Sage allows you go directly to the relevant nominal accounts to enter opening balances and makes the accounting entries for you. This can be a useful method to use for Task 3 in the assessment.

To enter opening balances on nominal accounts, choose **Company** and then find the nominal account you wish to add an opening balance to. For example you may want to post the opening balance for a property.

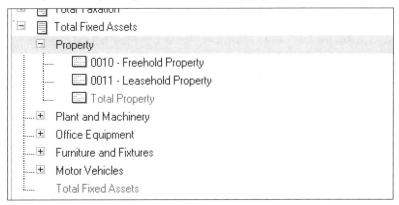

Selecting the account and clicking on **Nominal Record** brings up the following screen which includes a 'Balance' field near the top of the 'Details' tab.

Clicking on the small button to the right of this field marked '**OB**' brings up a screen where you can enter and save an opening balance (although don't save anything now).

Note that for any entries made using this option, the corresponding entry will be posted to a suspense account. However, since opening balances entered should sum to zero (having the same value of debits and credits), entering all opening balances should result in a zero balance overall on the suspense account.

Tax codes

When entering transactions it is important to use the appropriate tax code to ensure the VAT is correctly treated. The tax codes are summarised below.

Tax code	Used for
T0	Zero-rated transactions, such as books, magazines, and train fares. (Think of the code as 'T Zero' – then you will never confuse it with the code for exempt transactions).
T1	Standard rate, currently 20%. Some standard-rated items that catch people out are taxi fares (but only if the taxi driver is VAT-registered), restaurant meals, and stationery. You can only reclaim VAT if you have a valid VAT invoice; if not use code T9.
T2	Exempt transactions such as bank charges and insurance, postage stamps, professional subscriptions.

Tax code	Used for
T9	Transactions not involving VAT, for example wages, charitable donations, internal transfers between accounts (for instance from the bank to the petty cash account). Also used if the supplier is not VAT-registered or if you do not have a valid VAT invoice.

There are also codes for transactions with organisations in the EU (outside the UK), because these need to be shown separately on a VAT return, but these are outside the scope of this unit. You may also be aware that there is a reduced rate of 5% for certain things such as domestic electricity, but this does not normally apply to business expenditure.

The above examples cover everything you are likely to encounter in an assessment.

Editing VAT codes and rates

Occasionally new VAT rates such as the 5% rate are introduced or an existing VAT rate is changed. This happened when the rate moved from 17.5% to 20%. This easy to manage on Sage and only takes a few moments. The process is set out below and is for your general information. If you decide to try this out and change the VAT rate using the following steps, **make sure you change it back to 20% before you continue** through the Workbook. Alternatively click on **Cancel** at the end of Step 4 and do not click Save and your changes will not be saved.

Step 1   Click on Settings, and then select Configuration

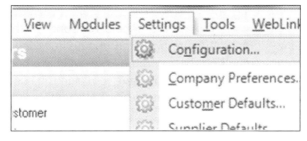

Step 2   Select the **tax codes** tab

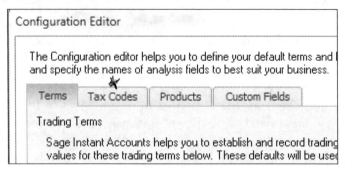

Step 3   In the tax codes tab you will find a list of tax codes. To change an exisiting code it is best to make the changes on the day it begins to affect your company or the nearest trading day after that, highlight the tax code on the list and then click on **Edit**.

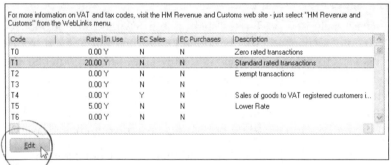

Step 4   The following pop-up screen appears. Simply overtype the existing rate with the new rate (this should be done on the day the rate changes). Once the rate has been updated clicking **OK** makes the pop-up screen disappear and the entry will have been amended in the tax code list. Clicking on **Save** results in the company tax code being updated but you should exit without clicking Save as we want to keep the VAT rate as 20%.

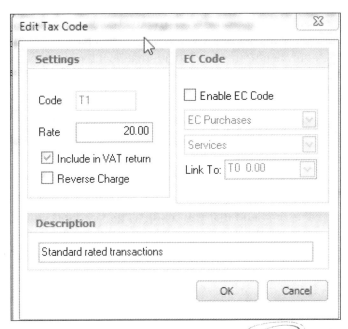

Some companies may prefer to run the older code and newer tax codes concurrently for a short while and in this case a new code will need to be created. To do this you would follow the instructions above but instead at Step Three a code should be selected that is currently unused (such as T3). The the older rate will be entered there, ensuring the **Include in VAT return** box is ticked. Step Four is unchanged.

If in doubt about which Tax code to use when creating new tax codes check with a manager or your accountant for advice as all companies are set up differently.

Trade and non-trade receivables

One thing to note is the Sage package does not make a distinction between trade and non-trade (or 'other') receivables; anyone to whom you grant credit is simply treated as a customer in Sage. (You can assign different types of customers to different categories and/or to different 'departments', but that is beyond the scope of your present studies.) Another point to note is that Sage uses UK terminology rather than IFRS terminology and therefore uses the term 'debtors' rather than 'receivables'. Therefore the receivables control account in Sage is named the debtors control account. You will **not** need to post non-trade or 'other' receivables so you will not need to use Sage's standard 'other debtors' account.

Important note: From now on we will use the same terminology as Sage uses (ie UK terminology) for the purposes of navigating through Sage. However please be aware of the equivalent terms used in international terminology. A list of these is provided at the front of this Workbook and it is the international terminology that will be used in any questions in tasks in your assessment.

CUSTOMER AND SUPPLIER DATA

Before you can post customer and supplier transactions you will also need to set up accounts in the trade receivables ledger (often referred to as the sales ledger) and the trade payables ledger (often referred to as the purchase ledger).

Once again we recommend that you set up all the accounts you need before you start posting any transactions.

In an assessment (and in real life) you will find the details you need on the documents you have to hand: the business's own sales invoices and its suppliers' purchase invoices.

Codes

The first decision you will need to make is what kind of codes to use. In Sage the default behaviour of the program, if you use the wizard to set up the new suppliers record, is to use the first eight characters (excluding spaces and punctuation) of the full name of the customer or supplier, so if you enter 'G.T. Summertown' as the name the package will suggest that you use the code GTSUMMER.

This is a very clear and easy to use coding system because the code actually contains information about the account to which it refers. If you just gave this customer the code '1' that may be fine when you only have a few customers, but if you have thousands it is most unlikely that you would know who, say, customer 5682 was, just from the code.

The program will not allow you to set up two customers or two suppliers with the same code, so if you had a customer called 'G. T. Summerfield' as well as one called 'G.T Summertown' you would get a warning message suggesting that you use the code GTSUMME1. For this reason many businesses actually introduce numbers into their coding systems. For example, you could use the first five letters of the name and then the numbers 001, 002 and so on for subsequent customers or suppliers with the same first five letters in their name (GTSUM001, GTSUM002, and so on).

Of course, in your work you would use the coding system prescribed by your organisation. However in an assessment you will usually be told which code to use. If a task does allow for choice, we recommend an alphanumeric system (a mixture of letters and numbers), as this displays your understanding of the need for understandable but unique codes.

Task 4

Do you think it is possible for a customer and a supplier to have exactly the same code? Explain your answer.

Entering the account details

We'll now illustrate setting up a supplier account. Please note that the process is identical for customers, apart from you will be working within the customer screens.

If you click the **Suppliers** button (bottom left of screen) this gives you a new set of buttons.

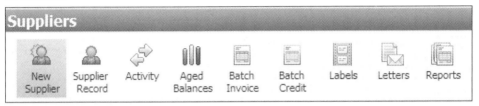

Note: If you don't see the labels (New Supplier, Supplier Record, Activity…) under each button then go to **Tools** > **Options** and tick **Show Text Labels** in **Toolbar**. If on clicking the **Supplier** button you see a graphic like the following, you can change the view to the buttons shown above by clicking on **Change View** and then selecting **Suppliers**.

To set up a new account you can click on **Supplier Record** and enter as many details as you have available. The details you need will usually be found on the supplier invoice. If the invoice shows an email address, for instance, be sure to type it in, even though you may not have email addresses for other suppliers. If you cannot find the relevant field try moving from tab to tab to find the field you want. Most information is entered in the first three tabs (Details, Defaults and Credit Control). Take care with typing, as always. When you are happy that everything is correct, click on **Save** and a blank record (like the one that follows) will now appear ready for you to enter the next record. Always remember to click **Save** after entering each supplier and when you are finished click on **Close**.

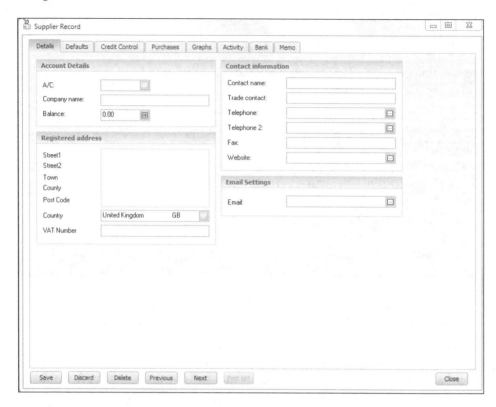

An alternative method for setting up a new account is to click on the **New Supplier** button and use the supplier record wizard to enter supplier details. Some people prefer to do this in the first instance although it can be slower and is not often used in the workplace. Try both methods and decide which is best for you.

Task 5

Set up a supplier account based on the following details taken from the heading of an invoice. Decide on an appropriate coding system yourself.

McAlistair Supplies Ltd
52 Foram Road
Winnesh
DR3 5TP
Tel: 06112 546772 Fax: 06112 546775
Email: sales@mcalisupps.co.uk
VAT No. 692 1473 29

If you use the wizard, don't put anything in for any other data, except for clicking on 'Terms Agreed' in the 'Credit details' screen.

Remember to **Save** the new account.

You will now see that McAlistair Supplies is now listed as a supplier in the main supplier window. Selecting McAlistair from the list then clicking on **Record** will bring up the following screen:

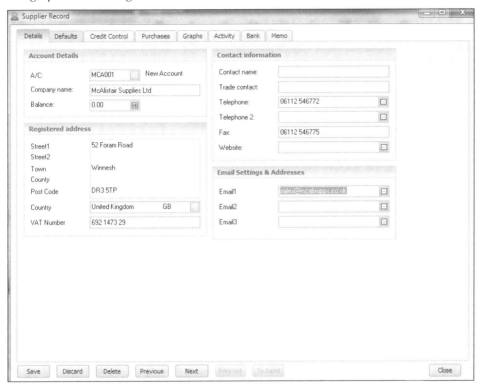

It is Important to note that you can enter an opening balance for the supplier in this screen by clicking on '**OB**' in the **Balance** field, once you have set up the supplier. The suppliers you are asked to set up in an assessment task may have opening balances and you can use the screen above to enter them.

If you see the following message when entering a supplier record:

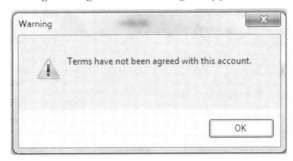

then click on the Credit Control tab for this record.

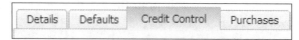

Put a tick in the appropriate checkbox at the foot of the screen, and then save the record. This is simply something Sage requires in order for you to continue entering data for this supplier/customer.

Restrictions

- [ ] Can charge credit
- [x] Terms agreed
- [ ] Restrict mailing
- [ ] Account On Hold

Customer and supplier defaults

By default, when you set up a new customer account the transactions you enter will be posted to the Debtors Control Account (debit gross amount), the Sales Tax Control Account (credit VAT amount) and the Sales Account (credit net amount).

Again, by default when you set up a new supplier account the transactions you enter will be posted to the Creditors Control Account (credit gross), the Purchase Tax Control Account (debit VAT) and the Purchases Account (debit net).

For sales, this is most probably exactly what you want to happen, unless you are specifically instructed that different types of sales should be posted to different sales accounts in the nominal ledger.

For purchases, however, for each supplier it would be better to set an appropriate default for the expense depending on the type of purchase. For example you would want to post a stationery supplier's invoices to the stationery account, but an insurance company's invoices to the insurance account.

To change the defaults, just open the supplier record and click on the **Defaults** tab.

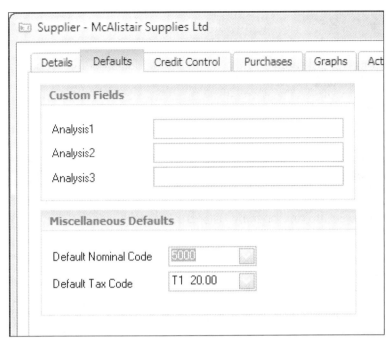

In the box labelled **Default Nominal Code** you can set the nominal ledger account to which all transactions with this supplier will be posted, unless you specify otherwise when you actually post a transaction. To see a list of all available accounts click on the arrow  at the right of the box or just press the F4 key on your keyboard. For example, we may wish to set the default for McAlistair Supplies to Publicity Material.

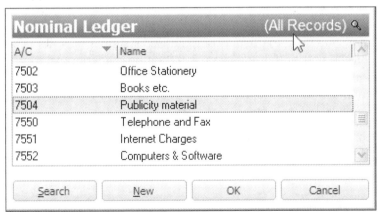

We could scroll down the list to the Publicity Material account created earlier (account 7504). If you need a new nominal account to post to, you can set one up from this screen – but we recommend using the wizard, as mentioned earlier.

Task 6

Open McAlistair Supplies Ltd suppliers record and set the default nominal code to 7504, Publicity Material.

Remember to **Save** this change.

JOURNALS

If you are setting up a new business the first entries you are likely to make will be done via a journal, to set up any opening balances (although see also the direct method covered earlier in this chapter for entering opening balances).

Journals are also used for non-routine transactions such as the correction of errors and recording drawings. You will be required to enter journals during your assessment in Task 11.

To post a journal in Sage click on the **Journal Entry** button shown when **Company** is chosen.

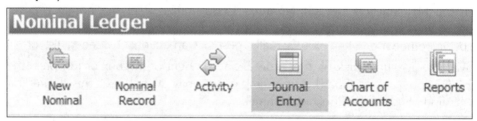

This journal entry screen looks reassuringly similar to a journal slip in a manual system, but all you need to do in a computerised system is fill in the slip and click on **Save**. All the entries to the 'books' will then be made in one go without any further effort from you. **Please Note:** Once saved or 'posted' it is not possible to correct a journal and you will need to input another journal to correct any errors so check carefully before saving.

Let's suppose you want to post the following journal, to set up the opening cash and capital balances.

DEBIT	Bank	2,750.00	
DEBIT	Petty Cash	250.00	
CREDIT	Capital		3,000.00

The Nominal Ledger journal input screen is shown below.

The table below explains what to do as you work through each entry field, in the order in which the TAB key will take you through them.

SCREEN ITEM	HOW IT WORKS
Reference	Type in the journal slip number you are given, if any. Journals should be numbered consecutively, so you may need to check to find out the number of the previous journal. If this is the first ever journal, choose your own coding system and make sure it has room for expansion. For example 'J001' allows for up to 999 journals in total.
Date	By default this field (box) will show the program date, but you should change it to 01/01/13. Pressing the F4 key, or clicking the ⬚ button will make a little calendar appear.
N/C	Enter the nominal ledger code of the account affected, or press F4 or click the ⬛ button to the right of this field to select from a list.
Name	This field will be filled in automatically by the program when you select the nominal code.
Ex. Ref	Leave this blank.
Details	Type in the journal narrative. In the second and subsequent lines you can press the F6 key when you reach this field, and the entry above will be copied without you needing to retype it. This can save lots of time.
T/C	The VAT code, if applicable. For journals this will almost invariably be T9 (transaction not involving VAT).
Debit/Credit	Type in the amounts in the correct columns. If it is a round sum, such as £250 there is no need to type in the decimal point and the extra zeros.

It is not possible to post a journal if it does not balance.

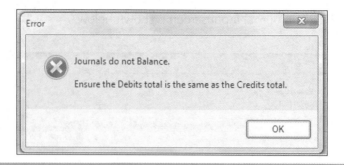

Task 7

Enter the journal shown earlier in the chapter (DR Bank 2,750, DR Petty Cash 250, CR Capital 3,000). Date it 01/01/13 and give a reference of JVI and tax code (T/C) 9. Enter 'Initial capital' in the details field. **Save** then **Close** the journal window.

If you click on **Company** you should see that 3,000 is listed against Total Current Assets and 3,000 listed against Total Capital & Reserves.

The importance of dates

By default, Sage sets the date of transactions to the current date according to your computer, but this may not be the date you want to use, especially if you are sitting an assessment.

It is vitally important to enter the correct date when you are using a computerised system, even if you are only doing a practice exercise, because the computer uses the date you enter in a variety of ways – to generate reports such as aged debtors reports, to reconcile VAT, and so on.

If you attempt to enter a date outside the financial year, you will see a warning such as the following.

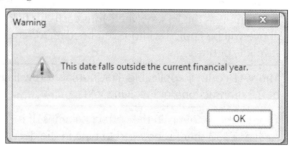

However, if you enter an incorrect date that falls within the financial year, Sage will allow you to do this.

The best way to avoid this kind of error, especially when undertaking an assessment, is to use the facility to set the program date before you enter any transactions. Select the **Settings** menu and then **Change Program Date**.

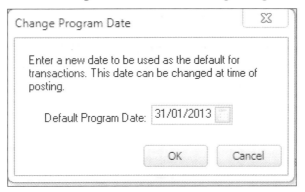

If you are doing an assessment we recommend that you set the program date to the last day of the month for which you are supposed to be posting transactions. That way you can never go seriously wrong.

Once you set the program date Sage will use it as the default date until you change it again or shut down the program. This has no adverse effect on any other programs you may be using and even within Sage the date will revert to the computer clock date the next time you use the program. Note that you will need to set the program date again if you shut down and then restart the program.

Task 8

Change the program date to 31 January 2013 and check that you have done so correctly by looking at the foot of the Sage screen.

Then close down the program (**File > Exit**). You should back-up your data when prompted to do so, using a file name that includes your own initials. You may need to ask your lecturer or manager where you should save the back-up file.

ENTERING INVOICES

You may be feeling that you have been working hard but not actually accomplished much yet! This is one of the few off-putting things about accounting packages: it can take quite a while to set everything up properly before you can really get started.

If you are feeling frustrated, just remember that you only have to set all these details up once. In future, the fact that all the data is available at the touch of a button will save you a vast amount of time, so it really is worth the initial effort.

Purchase invoices

Purchase invoices are created by your suppliers, whereas sales invoices are documents you create yourself. That means that it is usually simpler to enter purchase invoices so we'll deal with those first.

Having opened Sage, click on the **Suppliers** button (bottom left of screen), select a supplier, and then click on **Batch Invoice** on the Suppliers toolbar (change view to **Suppliers** if necessary).

As always, you can use the **TAB** key to move between different parts of the screen.

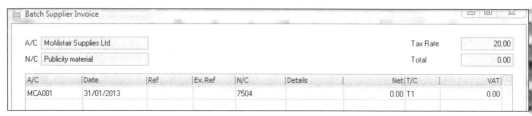

You can enter a number of different invoices from different suppliers on the same screen, and you can enter each line of an invoice separately. Obviously, you would need to do this if the invoice is for a variety of items that need to be coded to different nominal accounts.

To repeat the same entry in consecutive lines just press the **F6** key on your keyboard when you reach the appropriate field.

The following table explains what to do as you tab through each entry field. Pay particular attention to the **Net**, **T/C** and **VAT** fields.

SCREEN ITEM	HOW IT WORKS
A/C column	Select the supplier account from the drop down list (press the F4 key to see this, or click on the ⌄ button). The A/C box at the top left of the screen will show the full name of the supplier you select, so you can check to make sure you have the right one.
Date	The program date will be entered by default, but you can change this if you wish. Press F4 to see an on-screen calendar.
Ref	Type in the supplier's invoice number.
Ex. Ref	Leave this blank.
N/C	This will show the default code for this supplier (the N/C box at the top left of the screen will show the name of this account). If you need to change it press F4 or click the ⌄ button to see a list of nominal ledger accounts.

SCREEN ITEM	HOW IT WORKS
Details	Type in a brief but clear description of the item and be sure that your description will be understood by someone other than you. Usually you will just need to copy the description on the supplier's invoice.
Net	Enter the net amount of the invoice, excluding VAT. If the invoice has several lines you can enter each line separately but you should use the same Ref for each line.
	The ▢ button in this field will call up an on-screen calculator.
	Alternatively, type in the gross amount and press the **F9** key on your keyboard (or click Calc Net).
T/C	The VAT code, as explained earlier. Type in or select the appropriate code for the item.
VAT	This item will be calculated automatically, depending on the tax code selected. Check that it agrees with the VAT shown on the actual invoice. You can overtype the automatic amount, if necessary.

When you have entered all the invoice details you post them simply by clicking on **Save**. This will post ALL the required accounting entries to the ledgers.

Task 9

Post an invoice from McAlistair Supplies dated 6 January 2013 for 2000 sheets of A4 paper (net price: £20.35) and a box of 100 blue promotional biros (gross price: £10.00). The invoice number is PG45783. **Save** and **Close**.

Write down the total amount of VAT, as calculated by the program.

£_____

I don't believe it!

The first time you do this you will probably not quite believe that double entry to all the ledgers can be so incredibly easy. Check for yourself by looking at the individual accounts.

To check the nominal ledger click on the **Company** button (bottom left of the screen) then on **Nominal ledger** in the links section (alternatively you can click on the **Modules** menu and choose **Nominal ledger**).

Depending on which type of transaction you posted you should then select either the Debtors Ledger Control Account or the Creditors Ledger Control Account by expanding Total Current Assets or Total Current Liabilities using the '+' signs. Having selected the account you want, you should then double click on it.

Choose the **Activity** tab and you will see something like this.

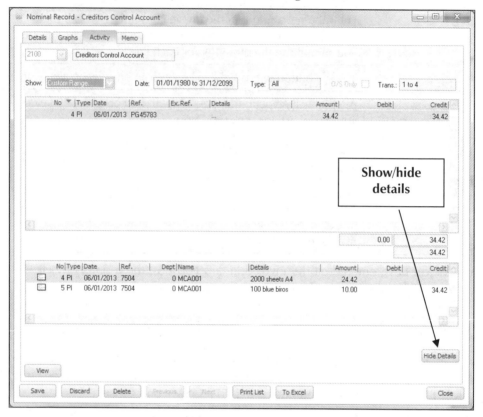

You can also click on the expense account in the nominal ledger and see the activities for that account.

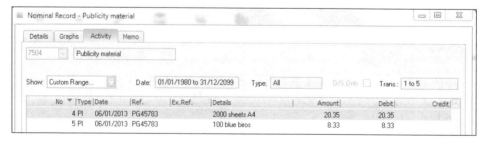

VAT was dealt with by a debit to the Purchase Tax Control Account.

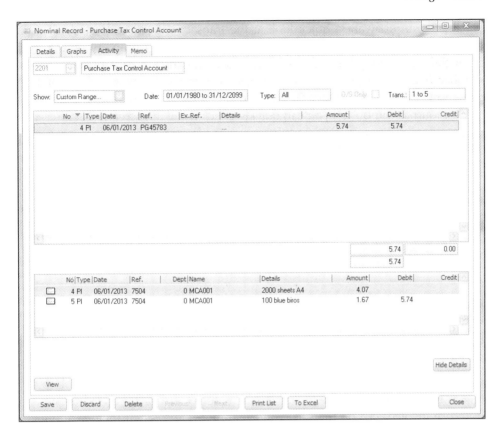

To check that the correct amounts have also been posted to the subsidiary ledger, simply open the record for the relevant customer or supplier and choose the **Activity** tab.

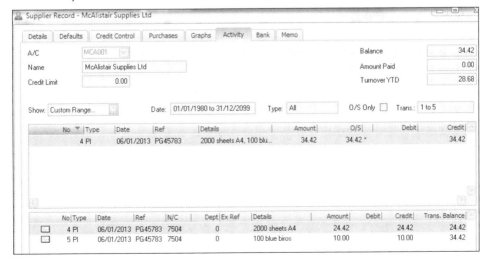

Finally, if you just want a quick look at the transactions you've posted, click on the **Modules** menu then select **Financials** (or press the **Company** button then **Financials** in **Links**). This will result in you being shown a list of transactions, numbered in the order in which you posted them. This can be very useful on certain occasions, for instance, if you can't remember the reference number of the last journal you posted you can quickly check using this screen.

Financials

No	Type	Account	Nominal	Details	Date	Ref	Ex.Ref	Net	Tax	T/C	Paid	Amount Paid	Bank
1	JD		1200	Initial capital	01/01/2013	JV1		2750.00	0.00	T9	Y	2750.00	N
2	JD		1230	Initial capital	01/01/2013	JV1		250.00	0.00	T9	Y	250.00	-
3	JC		3000	Initial capital	01/01/2013	JV1		3000.00	0.00	T9	Y	3000.00	-
4	PI	MCA001	7504	2000 sheets A4	06/01/2013	PG45783		20.35	4.07	T1	N	0.00	-
5	PI	MCA001	7504	100 blue biros	06/01/2013	PG45783		8.33	1.67	T1	N	0.00	-

Sales invoices if no invoice is produced

Some businesses create sales invoices using a different system from their accounts package – for example using word processing software such as Word. The invoices are then entered into the computerised accounting package.

If that is the case then sales invoices are entered in exactly the same way as purchase invoices. To do this, click on **Customers** then **Batch Invoice** and enter the invoices in a batch.

Sales invoices if the system creates the invoice

In Sage you can produce printable invoices that are automatically posted by Sage. If you wanted to do this, you could do so by clicking on **Customers** and then the **New Invoice** button under **Tasks**. The invoice details can then be entered, saved and an invoice printed.

However, in the assessment you will be given a list of invoices or sample invoices to enter. Therefore you should only enter invoices using the Batch Invoice method described earlier rather than creating an invoice.

Task 10

(1) Set up two more **suppliers** with the following details (using the new supplier wizard if you wish).

Widgets Unlimited Ltd
123 High Road
London
W23 2RG
020 8234 2345

Office Products Ltd
321 Low Road
London
E32 2GR
020 8432 5432

(2) Process the purchase of:

(a) 10 widgets (material purchased) from Widgets Unlimited Ltd for a total net cost of £80. Invoice number WU4474, dated 8 January 2013.

(b) A computer (office equipment) from Office Products Ltd for a net cost of £800. Invoice OP1231, dated 10 January 2013.

Both purchases attract VAT at the standard rate.

Task 11

(1) Set up a new **customer** with the following details (using the new customer wizard if you wish).

Alexander Ltd
501 Dart Road
Leeds
LS12 6TC
0113 2454 3241
info@alexander.co.uk
30 days' credit (payment due days)
All other fields can be left blank but tick the **terms agreed** option.

(2) Post the following two invoices (remember, you have to use '**Save**' to post them) to this customer:

(a) Invoice 001: Product: 10 widgets at a selling price (net) of £20 each. VAT to be charged at standard rate. Date 15 January 2013.

(b) Invoice 002: Service: Advice on widgets, at a fee of £50. VAT to be charged at standard rate. Date 25 January 2013.

(3) If you have not already done so, change the names of the nominal ledger accounts as necessary to accommodate the different sales types in (2).

Task 12

Preview a trial balance at this stage. Select **Company > Financials > Trial > Preview**, set month period to January 2013. (Note that 'Financials' appears in the Links section when company is selected.)

Date:	07/06/2013	SFE Merchandising		Page: 1
Time:	11:55:45	Period Trial Balance		

To Period: Month 1, January 2013

N/C	Name	Debit	Credit
0030	Office Equipment	800.00	
1100	Debtors Control Account	300.00	
1200	Bank Current Account	2,750.00	
1230	Petty Cash	250.00	
2100	Creditors Control Account		1,090.42
2200	Sales Tax Control Account		50.00
2201	Purchase Tax Control Account	181.74	
3000	Capital		3,000.00
4000	Sales - Products		200.00
4001	Sales - Services		50.00
5000	Materials Purchased	80.00	
7504	Publicity material	28.68	
	Totals:	4,390.42	4,390.42

Now take a second backup.

Credit notes

Supplier credit notes are posted in exactly the same way as supplier invoices except that you begin by clicking on **Supplier** and then the **Batch Credit** button, instead of the Batch Invoice button. The entries you make will appear in red, as a visual reminder that you are creating a credit note.

Customer credit notes can be posted in this way too.

PASSWORD PROTECTION

It is important to password protect confidential accounting data. In the assessment you are required to access the screen from which you would enter or change a password.

To set up or to change a password in Sage you select **Change Password** option from the **Settings** menu at the top of the screen.

This will bring up the following prompt if a password has not been set previously.

In the assessment, you will be told to simply select the appropriate option to enter or change a password. You will then need to print a screenshot of the screen shown above to prove you have selected the appropriate option.

In real life you would usually use this screen to set up a password, but in the assessment you will be told **not** to do so. There are examples of the task requiring you do access the password screens in the practice assessments at the back of this Workbook.

HELP!

Help in Sage

If ever you are unsure about how to perform a task in Sage, take a look in the built-in Help feature. Help is accessed via the menu, or by pressing the F1 key.

We recommend you explore the options shown under the Help menu. There are a number of useful guides on how to perform common tasks.

To search for a help on a specific topic, from the Help menu select **Contents and Index**.

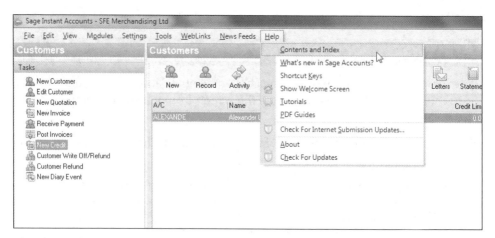

Then, use the Search function to find the topic you want help on. Experiment with this, the ability to find out how do something yourself could come in handy in your work and in your assessment.

Help from your manager and others

Whenever you are unsure about what to do, or are faced with an error message you are unsure about, the golden rule is **ask for help or advice**.

Don't ignore error messages. If possible, have your manager or someone more senior look at the message immediately and advise you what action to take. If you need to provide details to someone if they can't get to your screen to view it, take a screen print for them.

CHAPTER OVERVIEW

- Accounting packages range from simple bookkeeping tools to more complex packages. Sage's products are among the most popular packages in the UK

- Assessments may involve setting up new customer and supplier accounts, posting journals, invoices, payments and receipts, and producing printouts or other types of output

- It is essential to make sure that you are posting transactions to the correct financial year

- New nominal ledger accounts can be set up using the accounting package's 'wizard'

- VAT is dealt with by assigning the correct code to a transaction

- New customer and supplier accounts should be given consistent and meaningful codes

- Using the keyboard shortcuts may help you when you are entering data into Sage. The Tab key, the Esc key and the function keys (eg F4 and F6) can often speed up your work

- It is important to password protect confidential accounting data and in the assessment you need to be able to access the screen where you enter or change a password

- Familiarise yourself with the Help feature, it could come in handy both in your work and in your assessment

- Never ignore error messages, ask for help or advice from your manager

Keywords

Activity – the transactions that have occurred on an account

Back-up – a copy of a file created in case the original is lost or damaged

Chart of accounts – a template that sets out the nominal ledger accounts and how they are organised into different categories

Defaults – the entries that the accounting package expects to normally be made in a particular field

Field – a box on screen in which you enter data or select from a list (similar to a spreadsheet cell)

General ledger – the ledger containing the income statement (profit and loss) and statement of financial position (balance sheet) accounts

Nominal ledger – the term Sage uses for the ledger containing the income statement (profit and loss) and statement of financial position (balance sheet) accounts

Program date – the date Sage uses as the default for any transactions that are posted (the default may be overwritten)

Restore – the process of overwriting the data currently held in the program with back-up data

Tax code – Sage's term for the code to be used to calculate VAT

TEST YOUR LEARNING

Test 1

What is a 'field' in an accounting package?

Test 2

What do you understand by the term 'default'?

Test 3

Why do you think accounts codes are important in accounting packages?

Test 4

Before you shut down an accounting package it is essential to save your work. True or False? Explain your answer.

Test 5

What happens when you restore a back-up file?

Test 6

When is it not possible to change the financial year of an accounting package?

Test 7

Why is it important that details such as company name and address are entered with no mistakes or typing errors?

Test 8

What is a chart of accounts?

Test 9

In an accounting package there will usually be codes for at least four different types of transactions. What are these types?

Test 10

What must be done before a supplier credit invoice can be posted?

Test 11

How would a supplier invoice be assigned to the correct nominal ledger account?

Test 12

If you attempt to post a journal that does not balance the difference will be posted to the suspense account. True or False? Explain your answer.

Test 13

Why is it so important to enter the correct date for a transaction?

Test 14

If a purchase invoice has five separate lines should these be posted individually or is it sufficient just to post the invoice totals?

chapter 2:
SAGE – PART 2

chapter coverage 📖

The topics covered in this chapter follow on from where you should have reached in Chapter 1.

The subjects covered in this chapter are:

- ✍ Payments and receipts
- ✍ Bank reconciliations
- ✍ Print-outs and other types of output
- ✍ Error correction
- ✍ Month-end procedures

PAYMENTS AND RECEIPTS

Your assessment may include details of payments and receipts to enter into the accounts. These could comprise cash, cheques and automated payments.

You need to be able to distinguish between cheques that you have sent to suppliers and cheques received from customers. If it is a cheque that you have paid out to a supplier you may only be shown the cheque stub (that's all you would have in practice, after all), such as illustrated below.

```
┌─────────────────────────────────────┐
│                                     │
│   Date      ...........................  │
│                                     │
│   Payee     ...........................  │
│                                     │
│             ...........................  │
│                                     │
│             ...........................  │
│                                     │
│             ...........................  │
│                                     │
│   £         ...........................  │
│                                     │
│             000001                  │
│                                     │
└─────────────────────────────────────┘
```

If it is a cheque that you have received from a customer you may be shown the cheque itself.

```
┌─────────────────────────────────────────────────┐
│  Lloyds TSB                           30-92-10    │
│                                                   │
│  Benham Branch                    Date _____  │
│                                                   │
│  Pay_____         │
│                                          ┌──────┐ │
│  _____│      │ │
│                                          │      │ │
│                                          └──────┘ │
│  _____                  │
│                                                   │
│                          FOR WHITEHILL SUPERSTORES│
└─────────────────────────────────────────────────┘
```

You can tell that this is a receipt because the name below the signature (here Whitehill Superstores) will be the name of one of your customers.

In the assessment, you could also be given details of an electronic payment or receipt, for example a BACS remittance advice detailing a receipt from a customer.

Alternatively, you may be shown a paying-in slip that may include receipts from several different customers.

Cheques etc.			Brought forward £			£50		
						£20		
						£10		
						£5		
						£2		
						£1		
						50p		
						20p		
						Silver		
			Whitehill	1468	75	Bronze		
			Superstores			Total Cash		
						Cardnet		
			G T				3818	75
			Summerfield	2350	00	Cheques etc.		
Carried forward £			Carried forward £	3818	75	Total £	3818	75
Date 23/01/2010		500001	FOR SFE MERCHANDISING			06325143		

Supplier payments

When you pay a supplier it is important to allocate your payment to invoices shown as outstanding in the purchase ledger. Sage makes this very easy.

There are a number of different payments allocations that can occur in both the Sale and Purchase ledger. Usually you will pay most invoices in full or take a credit note in full, however there may be reasons why an invoice may only be partially paid, due to disputes or cash flow problems. These are unsurprisingly know as 'part payments'. Occasionally you may not be able to allocate a payment or receipt because it is for an invoice not on the system or the amount does not match with your ledger. In these cases the payment is recorded against the correct account but not to any particular invoice or credit note and these are known as 'payments on account'.

Discounts can be allowed or received, and a discount field is available to make a note of these amounts.

To post a payment to a supplier click on **Bank** on the main toolbar and then on the **Supplier Payment** button towards the top of the screen (NOT the **Bank Payments** button, which relates to payments not involving suppliers accounts).

You are presented with a screen that looks a little like a blank cheque with drop-down options which allow you to choose the bank account used for the payment and the supplier who is being paid.

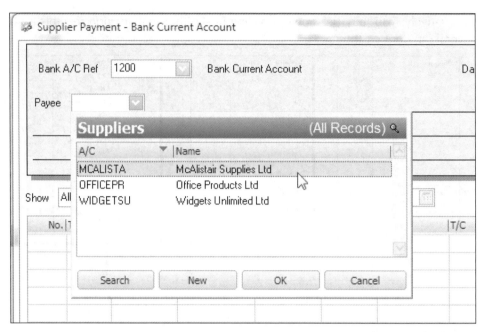

If you choose McAlistair Suppliers Ltd, the next screen completes some of the cheque, and the bottom half of the screen shows details of outstanding invoices.

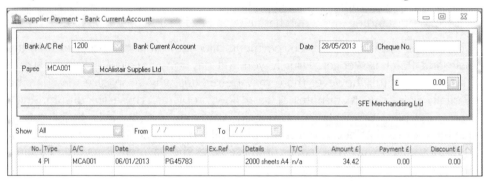

The following table explains the quickest way to post a payment to a supplier. Press Tab to move from one field to the next.

SCREEN ITEM	HOW IT WORKS
Payee	Select the code for the supplier you want to pay.
Date	The program date will be entered by default, but you can change this if you wish. Press F4 to see an on-screen calendar.
Cheque number	Enter this carefully as it will help with bank reconciliations.

SCREEN ITEM	HOW IT WORKS
£ box	Though it might seem odd, leave this at 0.00 when paying an invoice in full as it will automatically be filled in when we update the Payment £ box. Note: When processing a payment on account or unallocated payment you should enter the amount that will be allocated at a later date. On saving a warning screen will appear advising that you are making a payment on account. Such payments should be allocated as soon as the relevant information or invoice is available.
Payment £	Do not type anything here. Just click on the 'Pay in Full' button at the bottom of the screen. If there are several invoices to pay ensure you click into the payment field of the required invoice.
Discount	Tab past this if there is no discount. However if you do need to process a discount enter the discount amount in the discount field *first* and Sage will calculate the balance to be paid and enter it automatically into the payment field.
Save	This saves to ALL the ledgers.

Using this method the amount of the cheque, shown in the £ box in the top half of the screen, updates each time you click on Pay in Full. The program is also clever enough to write the amount in words.

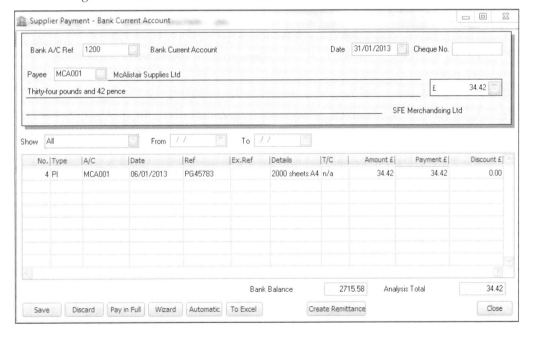

You don't need to pay all the outstanding invoices if you don't want to. You can just click on **Save** when you've paid the ones you want.

This is the quickest way of posting a payment in ordinary circumstances.

There may be times when you don't want to pay invoices in full. For instance, you may decide to pay the supplier in the illustration above only £50, because of some problem with the items supplied. In that case, proceed as follows.

SCREEN ITEM	HOW IT WORKS
Payee	As before
Date	As before
Cheque number	As before
£ box	Though it might seem odd, leave this at 0.00
Payment £	Type the amount you want to pay
Discount	Tab past this
Save	This saves to ALL the ledgers

A further possibility is that there will be a credit note on the account as well as invoices. **Pay in Full** is the answer to this, too. When you reach the credit note line click on **Pay in Full** and the amount of the cheque will be reduced by the correct amount.

Task 1

Post a payment on 31/01/13 made with cheque 158002 to McAlistair Supplies Ltd for the total of invoice PG45783. Remember to click '**Save**' to effect the posting.

When you post a supplier payment, you also have the option of generating and printing a remittance advice to be sent to the supplier to inform them of the invoices your company is paying. To do this, you use the **Create Remittance** Button after you have allocated the payment to an invoice or series of invoices. You may be asked to print a remittance during your assessment.

An example is given in the screen shot that follows, where a payment is allocated against an Office Products invoice we created in an earlier task. You can try this for yourself and generate a remittance, but for the purposes of progressing through this book, you should **not** save the payment.

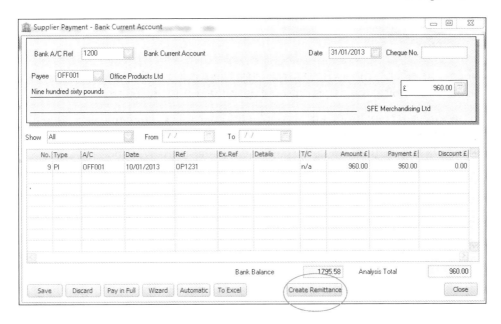

When you click on **Create Remittance** you will be given a choice of layouts. Selecting the default layout and pressing **Run** should result in a remittance similar to the one shown below. This can then be printed.

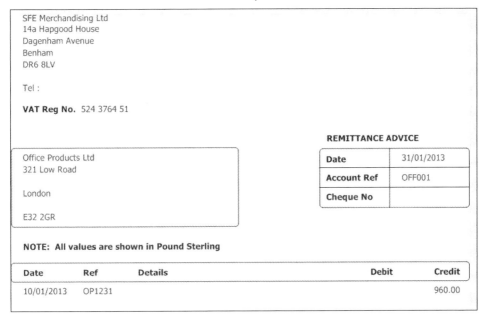

Customer receipts

When you receive money from your customers it is important to allocate your payment to invoices shown as outstanding in the subsidiary ledger.

To record a receipt from an account customer, click on **Bank** and then the **Customer Receipt** button towards the top of the screen (NOT the **Bank Receipts** button). Following that, select the customer you have received money from.

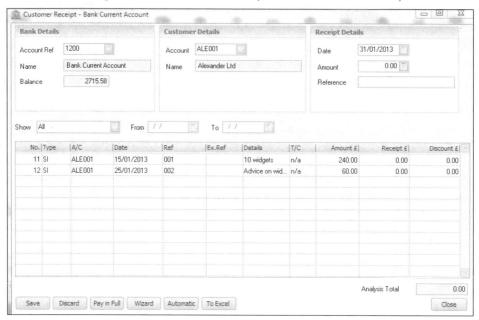

Although this screen looks slightly different from the payment one, it works in exactly the same way, and we recommend that you use it in exactly the same way – in other words, rely on the **Pay in Full** button unless dealing with unallocated payments or 'Payments on Account'.

One important point to remember when posting receipts is that you should use the paying-in slip number (if you have it) for the **Reference**. This makes it much easier to complete bank reconciliations, because typically several cheques will be paid in on a single paying-in slip and the bank statement will only show the total, not the individual amounts.

Task 2

Post a receipt from Alexander for £240. This was paid in using paying-in slip 500001 dated 31 January 2013. You should allocate this against Invoice 001.

Other payments and receipts

Some payments and receipts do not need to be allocated to customers or suppliers. Examples include payments like wages and receipts such as cash sales and VAT refunds.

If your assessment includes transactions like this you should post them by clicking on **Bank** and then **Bank Payments** (or **Bank** and then **Bank Receipts**).

Here's an example of how a loan from the bank might be posted to the accounts (don't carry out the transaction). Use the **N/C** drop-down to find which nominal code to use. Note that transactions like this will often not involve VAT, in which case the **T/C** code to use is T9.

The screen for posting payments such as wages is exactly the same but instead of using the Bank Receipts screen you access the payments screen through **Bank Payments**.

Direct debits and standing orders

Many businesses have regular recurring payments, such as rent or rates, set up by standing order or direct debit. It can be easy to forget to post these – especially as some may be monthly, some quarterly and so on. Sage makes it easy to automate this process. Choosing **Bank** > **Recurring Items** > **Add** will produce a screen like the one that follows. It allows you to specify:

- The type of transaction
- Where the debit is to be posted
- Start date
- Frequency
- End date
- Amounts (gross/net/VAT)

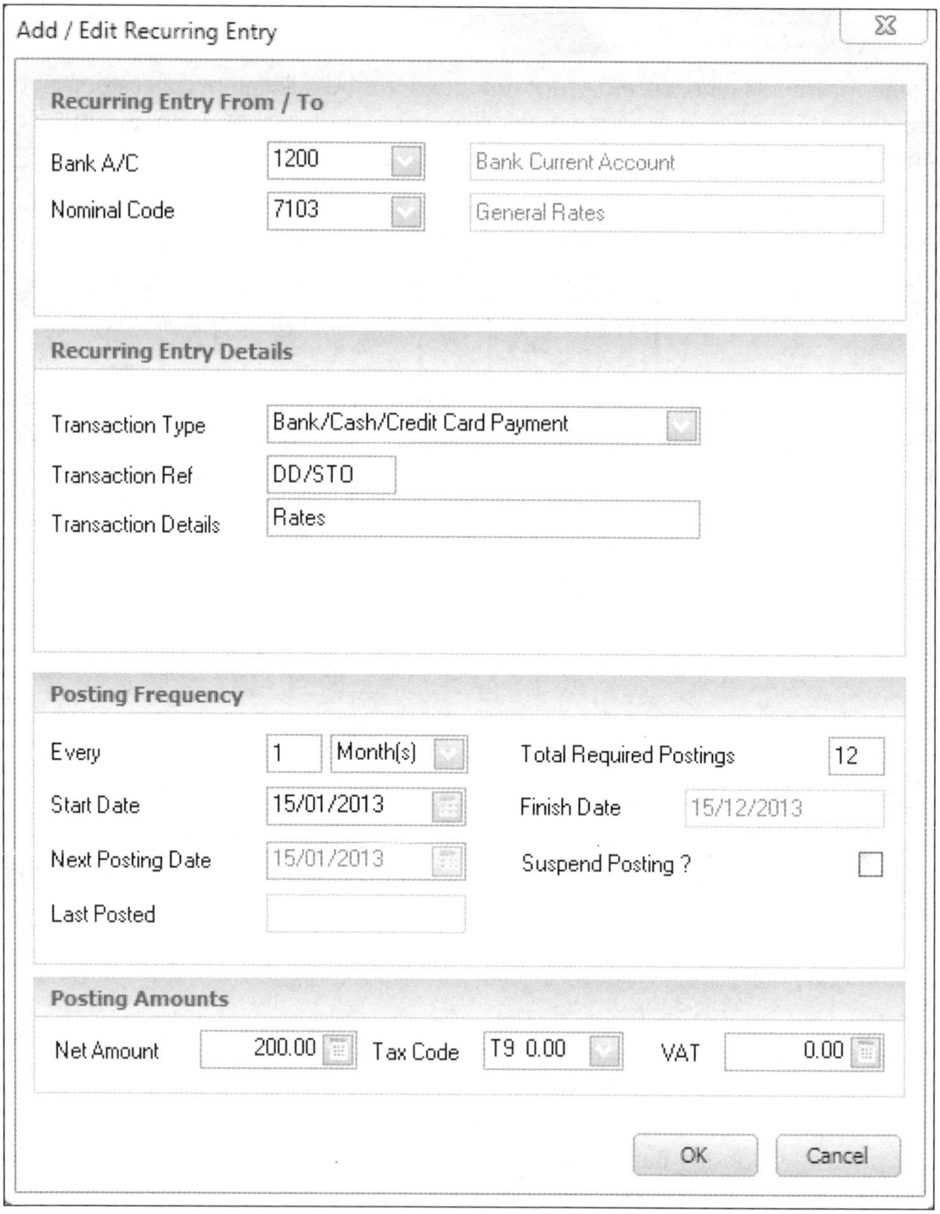

Add / Edit Recurring Entry	⚔

Recurring Entry From / To

Bank A/C	1200	▽	Bank Current Account
Nominal Code	7103	▽	General Rates

Recurring Entry Details

Transaction Type	Bank/Cash/Credit Card Payment ▽
Transaction Ref	DD/STO
Transaction Details	Rates

Posting Frequency

Every	1	Month(s) ▽	Total Required Postings	12
Start Date	15/01/2013		Finish Date	15/12/2013
Next Posting Date	15/01/2013		Suspend Posting ?	☐
Last Posted				

Posting Amounts

Net Amount	200.00	Tax Code	T9 0.00 ▽	VAT	0.00

OK	Cancel

The above shows how the details of a regular monthly payment for rates could be entered. Changing the reference can indicate whether it is a standing order or a direct debit. Note that you may be asked to screen print the screen above during the assessment as evidence of you setting up a recurring entry.

Task 3

Enter and save the recurring rates payment details shown above.

BPP
LEARNING MEDIA

Although the details for recurring payments are now saved, no transactions have been posted. To make the entries you have to now choose **Bank > Recurring Items** to bring up the following screen.

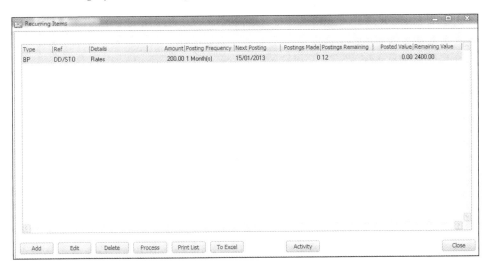

Then you select the relevant series of payments and click on the **Process** button to bring up any recurring payments up to the program date (which was set as 31 January 2013 earlier).

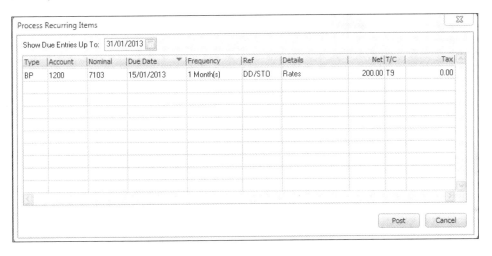

Don't do it now (wait for the next task!), but you can post the payment(s) shown by pressing the **Post** button. You can show and post later or all payments by changing the 'Show Due Entries Up To' date at the top. However you will only want to post those payments that you expect to go through the bank in the month you are accounting for.

Task 4

Use the recurring payments option to post the rates payment of £200 for **January 2013 only**.

Once you have posted a payment or payments you should notice the Recurring Items screen shows that a payment or payments have been posted in the 'Postings Made' column.

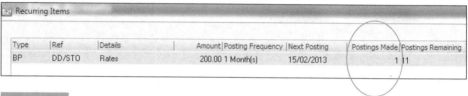

Petty cash

Petty cash transactions are posted in exactly the same way as bank transactions except that you use the Petty Cash bank account rather than the Bank Current Account. As always, take care to use the correct VAT code.

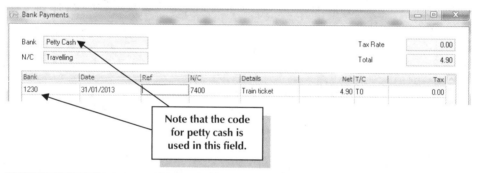

BANK RECONCILIATIONS

To access the bank reconciliation screens you need to click on **Bank** and then select the account you want to reconcile. In Sage the default bank current account is account 1200 so you can select this and then click on **Reconcile**. This brings up a statement summary screen.

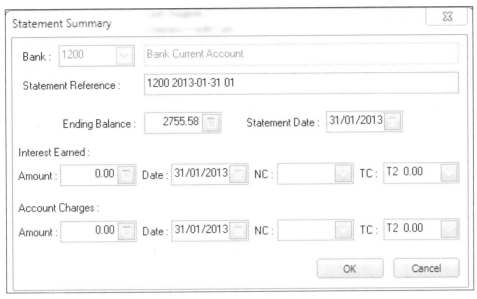

This screen gives you a first opportunity to enter the statement reference, balance and date and to enter any interest or charges appearing on the statement not yet entered in the records. The ending balance that automatically comes up is the balance on the nominal account, so should be updated to the balance shown on the statement.

Say that the closing bank statement balance is £2,790.00. That information would be entered in the **Ending Balance** box of the Statement Summary screen. If the statement is dated 31/01/2013 that can be entered in the **Statement Date** box.

If you forget to update the statement balance or any other details, you can also update them in the next screen (the bank reconciliation screen). Adjustments for interest can also be made there.

When you click **OK** you are taken to the **Bank Reconciliation** screen that follows.

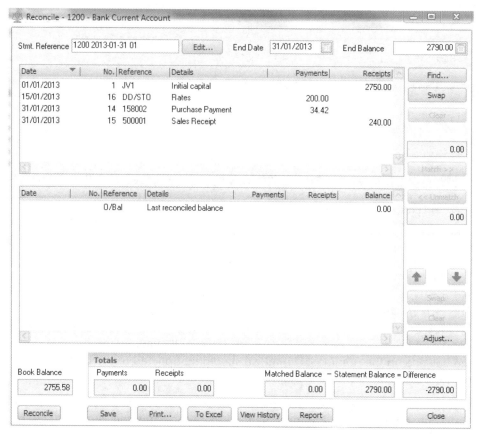

Initially, all cash account amounts are unmatched (you can see the matched balance box at the bottom shows zero), but by looking at the statement, some will be found to appear there also. We can match these items. Say that the initial journal of £2,750 into the bank account, the rates payment of £200.00 and the receipt of £240 from Alexander Ltd are also on the bank statement.

These can be selected and matched by clicking on the transaction and then on **Match >>** (note if you accidentally match the wrong entry then you can use **<< Unmatch** to go back a step). The statement screen will then look as follows:

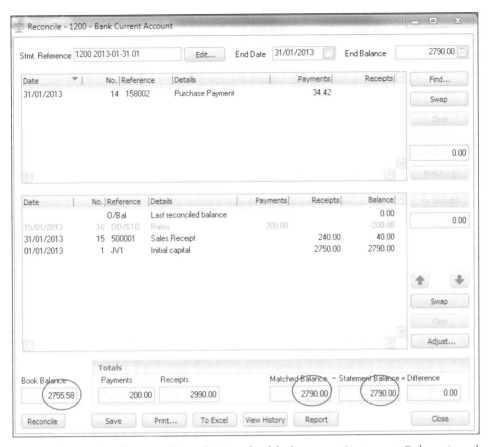

Reconciliation has been achieved! (Matched balance = Statement Balance) and the unmatched item of £34.42 explains the difference between the statement balance of £2,790.00 and the Sage bank current account balance (Book Balance) of £2,755.58.

The fields you enter in the Bank Reconciliation screen are as follows:

SCREEN ITEM	HOW IT WORKS
Date	Set this to the same date as the date of the statement received from the bank (probably the date of the last transaction shown on the statement).
Statement End Balance	Type in the closing balance on the bank statement, using a minus sign if the account is overdrawn.
Difference	This field is updated by the program as you select transactions on screen. The aim is to make this box show 0.00.

Task 5

Carry out the bank reconciliation explained in this section assuming that the closing bank statement balance is £2,790.

Although we look at reports in detail later in the chapter, at this stage it is worth pointing out you can generate a bank reconciliation report (a bank reconciliation statement) from the Bank Reconciliation screen. Clicking on **Report** should yield a report like the one shown below.

Bank Ref:	1200			Date To:	31/01/2013	
Bank Name:	Bank Current Account			Statement Ref:	1200 2013-01-31 02	
Currency:	Pound Sterling					

Balance as per cash book at 31/01/2013: 2,755.58

Add: Unpresented Payments

Tran No	Date	Ref	Details	£
17	31/01/2013	158002	Purchase Payment	34.42
				34.42

Less: Outstanding Receipts

Tran No	Date	Ref	Details	£
				0.00

Reconciled balance :	2,790.00
Balance as per statement :	2,790.00
Difference :	0.00

Adjustments

Even if you have posted all your transactions correctly there is a good chance that there will be items on the bank statement that you have not included in the accounts. Bank charges and interest are common examples.

For such items click on the **Adjust...** button on the bank reconciliation screen, select the type of adjustment to bring up the related adjustment screen (for earlier versions of Sage you may be taken straight to a general adjustments screen and will not have the option of also posting supplier and customer payments at this stage).

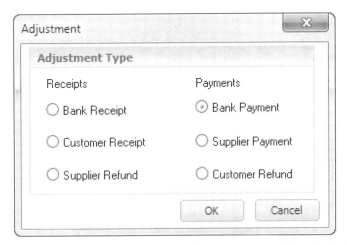

The adjustment screen allows you to enter the amounts and details before Saving. **Note**: For our purposes, **do not** carry out the following adjustment.

Make sure you use the correct tax code when making adjustments.

Note: On earlier versions of Sage, where you are taken straight to an adjustment screen, you may not be able to use this method to post payments to or receipts from credit suppliers or customers because the subsidiary ledgers will not be updated.

Grouped receipts

As we mentioned earlier, businesses often pay several cheques into the bank on the same paying-in slip and bank statements only show the total of the paying-in slip, not the individual items.

If you use the paying-in slip number as the **Reference** when posting receipts, Sage will allow you to group similar items together when doing a bank reconciliation. This may make it easier to agree them to the bank statement entries.

Within **Bank Defaults** in the **Settings** menu is a tick box called **Group items in Bank Rec**. When this is ticked consecutive transactions of the same type are combined as one item for display in the Bank Reconciliation screen if the reference and the date are the same.

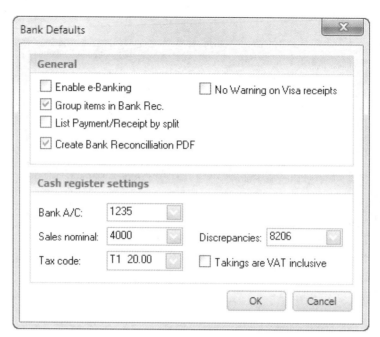

Some versions of Sage have an additional tick box called **Group Bank Transactions**.

If this check box within Bank Defaults is selected, bank transactions (bank payments and bank receipts) with the same reference and transaction date are grouped together within bank activity.

To see the individual transactions that make up the header, you must use the drill-down facility.

If you do not want your bank transactions to be grouped together in, clear the check boxes related to grouping items. When you clear the check boxes, each bank transaction appears on a separate line of the Bank Activity.

PRINT-OUTS AND OTHER TYPES OF OUTPUT

The importance of reports generated by the accounting systems

One of the most important features of an accounting system such as Sage is its ability provide a range of useful accounting information very quickly. If transactions are entered correctly in the first instance, then accurate summaries or detailed analysis should be available at the click of a button.

This is very important for both managers and accounts staff who depend on this information to make important decisions. The instant collation and reporting of the financial information they need enables them to make better informed decisions more quickly.

The information needed by each individual in the business will vary depending on their role and the situation they find themselves in. Management may focus more on the summaries to gain an understanding of 'the big picture' while finance staff will typically need to look at the more detailed reports.

To give a simple example of the use of a report by finance staff; the aged receivables analysis can be generated from Sage (as we will see later) and this will show how old each customer balance is. This will alert staff in charge of credit control to those accounts that are overdue and need chasing for payment, without them having to look back at the invoice dates.

The majority of the reports we will look at are usually produced periodically and used to check on the accuracy of the records.

We look at generating a nominal activity report later, which details all the transactions in a period in each account. A quick review of this report can help to identify errors, for example transactions posted to the wrong account. The trial balance generated by the accounting system may also highlight errors, for example if a suspense account has been set up and not yet been cleared.

We looked at bank reconciliations earlier and checking the related report against the bank statements is an important procedure that should be carried out regularly.

The various reports can also used to gain an overview of different financial areas and as a tool when dealing with customers and suppliers. Areas focussed on might include identifying and dealing with overdue customer invoices (aged receivables analysis), seeing which suppliers due for payment (payables listings) and establishing the cash available to the business to meet its commitments (bank related reports).

Another advantage of accounting systems is that they often contain standard templates of documents the business needs to send to customers and suppliers. For example Sage will use its built in standard templates to produce customer invoices, statements and letters. It does this by populating the standard document with the details previously entered into the accounting system, such as the customer name and address entered when the customer was first set up.

Generating reports

When you have finished entering transactions, the final task in your assessment will be to print out (or generate) some reports.

Sage offers you a large number of different standard reports. You can also create others of your own if you wish, containing the information you choose. Although the pre-prepared reports that are available in Sage don't all have names that you will immediately recognise from your knowledge of manual accounting systems,

rest assured that everything you are likely to be asked to produce in a assessment can easily be found.

One or two print-outs, such as customer statements, have their own buttons, but in general, to generate and then print a report, you open the part of the program you want a report on and choose the **Reports** button which usually appears on the far right hand side. The report button within **Customers** is found here:

Here's an example of the range of Customers reports that you could print. To get to this screen click on **Customers** then **Reports**. By clicking on each folder you can see the reports available for each category. Remember, Sage uses UK terminology but in your assessment you will be asked for reports named using international terminology. For example you may be asked for an 'aged trade receivables analysis' which will be called an 'aged debtors analysis' in the Sage reporting area.

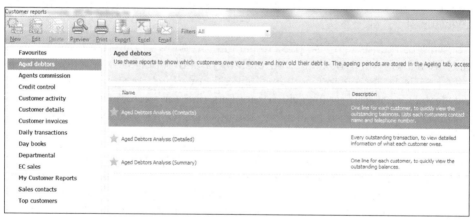

In recent versions of Sage the reports are organised into separate sections by subject, as shown in the illustration. In older versions this screen is laid out slightly differently, listing reports in folders or individually in alphabetical order. When you have found your report, select it.

The next step is to select the type of output you require. On this latest version you can select to preview, print, export or e-mail or save the report by using the buttons at the top of the screen.

Use **Print** to send the print-out to a printer – you will have the opportunity to select the printer you require.

Preview allows you to take a look at what will be printed out on screen before actually sending it to the printer. Use preview to ensure you have produced the correct report before printing hard copy.

Use **Export** to export to your computer for use in other programs (other than excel – see below). The default file type is often **PDF** and where you are asked to print reports for the assessment, PDFs can be generated as an alternative to hard copy prints. **Your assessor will tell you whether to hard copy print or to generate PDFs where the assessment tasks ask you to print reports**.

Use **Excel** to export the report ready for opening later in Excel. You will have the opportunity to select from a range of file types to create. This can be useful if you wish to send an Aged Debtors analysis to Excel.

Use **Email** to send the report directly via your computer's email program. This option is useful to send customer statements out using email.

When you have selected the appropriate button a screen will appear prompting you to enter the criteria for the report. The screen shot below shows the criteria specification screen that would be displayed if you were producing a supplier activity report (accessed within supplier reports).

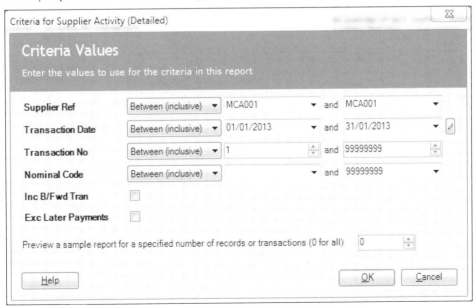

The default settings will produce a report on ALL supplier accounts up until the date specified unless you have selected a supplier. If you wish you can specify that you only want a report on a specific account (as in the preceding example), or range of accounts, by making selections in the **Supplier Ref** boxes. You can also restrict your report to cover a specific period by making entries in the **Transaction Date** boxes.

Ensure the transaction date range you specify covers all the transactions you need to see.

After clicking OK, assuming you selected the **Preview** option, the preview will appear on screen. Have a look through and, if you are happy that it shows the information you want, click the **Print** button.

Here is the report generated for **supplier** activity based on the information from the screen shown on the previous page.

Date: 07/06/2013				**SFE Merchandising**						**Page:** 1		
Time: 15:05:22				**Supplier Activity (Detailed)**								

Date From:	01/01/2013						Supplier From:	MAC001
Date To:	31/01/2013						Supplier To:	MAC001
Transaction From:	1						N/C From:	
Transaction To:	99,999,999						N/C To:	99999999
Inc b/fwd transaction:	No						Dept From:	0
Exc later payment:	No						Dept To:	999

** NOTE: All report values are shown in Base Currency, unless otherwise indicated **

A/C:	MAC001	Name:	McAlistair Supplies Ltd		Contact:			Tel:	06112 546772

No	Type	Date	Ref	N/C	Details	Dept	T/C	Value	O/S	Debit	Credit	V	B
4	PI	06/01/2013	PG45783	7504	2000 sheets A4	0	T1	24.42	0.00		24.42	N	-
5	PI	06/01/2013	PG45783	7504	100 blue biros	0	T1	10.00	0.00		10.00	N	-
17	PP	31/01/2013	158002	1200	Purchase Payment	0	T9	34.42	0.00	34.42		-	N
					Totals:			0.00	0.00	34.42	34.42		

Amount Outstanding	0.00
Amount paid this period	34.42
Credit Limit £	0.00
Turnover YTD	28.68

Here is an example of a **customer** activity report:

					SFE Merchandising							Page:	1	

Date:
Time:

SFE Merchandising
Customer Activity (Detailed)

Page: 1

Date From:	01/01/2013		Customer From:	ALE001
Date To:	31/01/2013		Customer To:	ALE001
Transaction From:	1		N/C From:	
Transaction To:	99,999,999		N/C To:	99999999
Inc b/fwd transaction:	No		Dept From:	0
Exc later payment:	No		Dept To:	999

** NOTE: All report values are shown in Base Currency, unless otherwise indicated **

A/C:	ALE001	Name:	Alexander Ltd		Contact:			Tel:	0113 2454 3241

No	Type	Date	Ref	N/C	Details	Dept	T/C	Value	O/S	Debit	Credit	V	B
8	SI	15/01/2013	001	4000	10 widgets	0	T1	240.00		240.00		N	-
9	SI	25/01/2013	002	4001	Advice on widgets	0	T1	60.00 *	60.00	60.00		N	-
18	SR	31/01/2013		1200	Sales Receipt	0	T9	240.00			240.00	-	N
							Totals:	60.00	60.00	300.00	240.00		

Amount Outstanding	60.00
Amount Paid this period	240.00
Credit Limit £	0.00
Turnover YTD	250.00

Invoices and statements

Some print-outs, such as invoices and statements, may be intended to be printed on pre-printed stationery. Remember that when you preview these documents on-screen, you will see words and figures on plain paper. This is obvious if you think about it, but we mention it because it surprises some new users.

To produce a customer statement you select the customer and click on the **Statements** button within Customers.

You then click on **Layouts** to bring up a series of different styles of statement.

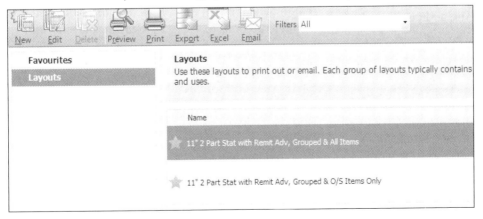

Using the first (default) option and clicking on **Preview** will bring up a menu where you can specify transaction dates before pressing **OK** generate a conventional statement. An extract of such a statement follows and the statement can be printed or exported as appropriate.

SFE Merchandising
14a Hapgood House
Dagenham Avenue
Benham
DR6 8LV

ALE001

Alexander Ltd   31/01/2013
501 Dart Road

Leeds

LS12 6TC

All values are shown in Pound Sterling

15/01/2013	001	Goods/Services	£	240.00		£	240.00
25/01/2013	002	Goods/Services	£	60.00		£	300.00
31/01/2013		Payment			£ 240.00	£	60.00

Print-outs in assessments

The following table lists the print-outs you may be asked for in an assessment with brief instructions explaining how to obtain them in Sage.

PRINT-OUT	HOW TO GET IT	WHICH REPORT TO CHOOSE
Audit trail The audit trail is where Sage stores all of the transactions that you enter. The audit trail is so called because it is a complete record of your transaction activities and is often requested by auditors during their investigations.	Click on **Modules**, select **Financials**, then on the **Audit Trail** button. Note that you can clear the audit trail (eg as part of the year end routine). This removes fully paid up and reconciled transactions, which speeds up program operation. It is vital to print the audit trail before clearing it.	*Detailed* type of audit trail with **Landscape Output**. Click on **Run** when you are asked for **Criteria** and you will get a list of ALL transactions in the order in which they were posted

PRINT-OUT	HOW TO GET IT	WHICH REPORT TO CHOOSE
Remittance advice	Please refer to the Supplier Payments section earlier in this chapter for details of how to generate and print a remittance.	Please see details of this earlier in this chapter
Customer statements	Click on the **Customers** button and then the **Statement** button.	*Stat with Tear Off Remit Adv. Grouped & All Items*
Bank reconciliation statement	Please refer back to the Bank Reconciliations section of this chapter to see how to generate a bank reconciliation statement. Note that the audit trail will show details of items reconciled via the bank reconciliation.	*Report within the Bank Reconciliation Screen*
Sales and Sales Returns Day Books	Click on **Customers**, then **Reports** and then click on **Day books**.	*Day Books: Customer Invoices (Detailed) Day Books: Customer Credits (Detailed)*
Purchases and Purchases Returns Day Books	Click on **Suppliers**, then **Reports** and then click on **Day books**.	*Day Books: Supplier Invoices (Detailed) Day Books: Supplier Credits (Detailed)*
Journal Day Book	Click on **Company**, then **Reports** and then click on **Day books**.	*Day Books: Nominal Ledger*
All sales ledger accounts (customer accounts) (showing all transactions within each account)	Click on **Customers**, then **Reports** and then click on **Customer Activity**.	*Customer Activity (Detailed)*

PRINT-OUT	HOW TO GET IT	WHICH REPORT TO CHOOSE
All purchases ledger (supplier) accounts (showing all transactions within each account)	Click on **Suppliers**, then **Reports** and then click on **Supplier Activity**.	*Supplier Activity (Detailed)*
Aged trade receivables/trade payables reports	Click on **Suppliers** or **Customers** as appropriate, then select **Aged debtors** or **Aged creditors**.	*Choose (and preview) the appropriate aged debtor/creditor reports*
Bank accounts	Click on **Banks**, then **Reports** and choose bank payments, bank receipts etc.	*Bank > cash payments* *Bank > cash receipts etc*
Nominal ledger accounts (showing all transactions within each account)	Click on **Modules**, then **Nominal ledger**, **Reports** and then on **Nominal Activity**.	*Nominal Activity – See note below*
Trial Balance	Click on **Modules** and select **Financials**, then click on the **Trial Balance** button.	*Choose Printer when asked about Print Output, unless you only want to preview the report*

Note:

For Nominal Activity reports you can set the criteria using the screen that follows to include one account, a range of accounts or all accounts. To include all accounts just leave the Nominal Code fields blank. To print one account, just enter/select the same account code in both Nominal Code fields as shown in the following screen print.

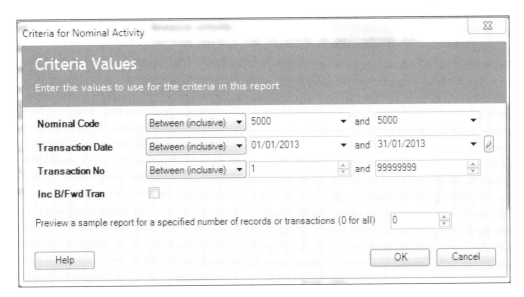

Task 6

Set up another customer as follows:

Springsteen Ltd
223 Home Town
Bradford
BD11 3EE

Process an invoice, Invoice 003, to this customer for £600 (net) for 20 Super-widgets, VAT at standard rate, invoice dated 26 January 2013.

Task 7

You notice that on 15 January the bank has debited your account £10 for bank charges (no VAT). Process this to the bank account, debiting the Bank Charges account in the nominal ledger.

On 31 January the bank credits you with £0.54 interest (no VAT). Rather than net this off against Bank interest charges, you decide to set up a new nominal ledger account: Bank interest received, in the Other sales category, account number 4906. Set up the new account and enter the interest received.

Exporting reports to PDF

The AAT Guidance for this unit states that instead of printing reports, reports PDF documents may be generated instead during the assessment. Your assessor will specify which method to use but here we cover how to export a report to PDF in case you need to use that method.

As mentioned earlier in the chapter, having selected a report there are a range of options for the method of output, including the **Export** option.

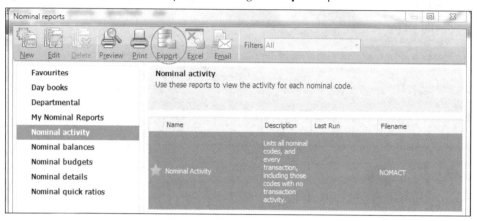

Using a nominal activity report as an example, clicking on **Export** will bring up the following screen (note that you can preview first using **Preview** if you wish):

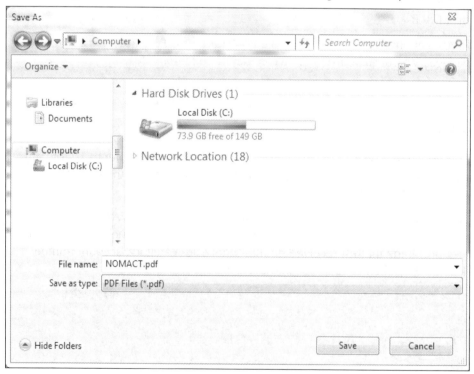

As you can see the default file type is PDF and the computer suggests a name for your file. You can rename this file and specify the location in which the PDF file containing your report is saved. If you then click on **Save** a PDF version of the report is created in your specified location.

Task 8

Ensure that the program data is set to 31/01/2013. Go to **Customers > Reports > Aged Debtors**.

From the **Aged Debtors** report list, select the Aged Debtors Analysis (Contacts).

Export the report to a specified location using the criteria offered, and a PDF version report will be saved.

Open the PDF version and review your report. It should show all invoices as current.

Transfers

To transfer between bank accounts (including petty cash) you use the **Bank Transfer** button or the **Bank Transfer** option from the appropriate **Task** menu. For example, to transfer £100 from the Bank Current Account to the Petty Cash account select **Bank** from the menu on the bottom left, then **Bank Transfer** from the task list.

Task 9

On 23 January, you transfer £100 from the bank account into petty cash and immediately spend:

- £20 on train fares (zero rated for VAT)

- £10 (gross amount) on coffee mugs for the office (standard rated). The net cost of the cups should be debited to Sundry Expenses

Remember, you can use F6 to repeat entries from the previous line.

Task 10

Extract a trial balance dated 31/01/2013 and back-up your data again.

If you wish you can also preview a statement of financial position (balance sheet) and statement of profit or loss (profit and loss account). You will not have to do this in your case study, but they are easy documents to produce and it seems a pity not to have a look!

Modules > Financials > Balance for the balance sheet

Modules > Financial > P and L for the profit and loss account

Your trial balance in Task 10 should look similar to the one that follows:

N/C	Name	Debit	Credit
Date: 07/06/2013	**SFE Merchandising**		**Page:** 1
Time: 15:49:22	**Period Trial Balance**		

To Period: Month 1, January 2013

N/C	Name	Debit	Credit
0030	Office Equipment	800.00	
1100	Debtors Control Account	780.00	
1200	Bank Current Account	2,646.12	
1230	Petty Cash	320.00	
2100	Creditors Control Account		1,056.00
2200	Sales Tax Control Account		170.00
2201	Purchase Tax Control Account	183.41	
3000	Capital		3,000.00
4000	Sales - Products		800.00
4001	Sales - Services		50.00
4906	Bank interest received		0.54
5000	Materials Purchased	80.00	
7103	General Rates	200.00	
7400	Travelling	20.00	
7504	Publicity material	28.68	
7901	Bank Charges	10.00	
8250	Sundry Expenses	8.33	
	Totals:	5,076.54	5,076.54

ERROR CORRECTION

If you make an error when you are making your entries it is relatively easy to correct.

Errors made when setting up customer and supplier accounts can be corrected simply by opening the relevant record and changing the data.

Errors made when typing in the details of a transaction (references, descriptions etc) can be corrected by clicking on the **File** menu and then on **Maintenance > Corrections**. A list of all the transactions you have posted so far will appear and you can select the one you want to change and click on **Edit Item**. When the record appears you can click on **Edit** and change the details as appropriate.

```
┌─────────────────────────────────────────────────────────────────────┐
│ Number 22, Cash Payment                                          ✕   │
├─────────────────────────────────────────────────────────────────────┤
│  Cash Payment Details                                                 │
│                                                                       │
│  N/C        ┌─────────────┬───┐                                       │
│             │ 7400        │ ▾ │                                       │
│             └─────────────┴───┘                                       │
│  Details    ┌──────────────────────────────────────────────────────┐ │
│             │ Train ticket                                         │ │
│             └──────────────────────────────────────────────────────┘ │
│  Date       ┌─────────────────┐                                       │
│             │ 23/01/2013      │                                       │
│             └─────────────────┘                                       │
│                                                                       │
│  Ex.Ref     ┌─────────────────┐                                       │
│             │                 │                                       │
│             └─────────────────┘                                       │
│                                                                       │
│  Net        ┌───────────┬──┐         T/C    ┌──────────────┬───┐      │
│             │    20.00  │▦ │                │ T0 0.00      │ ▾ │      │
│             └───────────┴──┘                └──────────────┴───┘      │
│  Tax        ┌───────────┬──┐         Paid   ┌───────────┬──┐          │
│             │     0.00  │▦ │                │    20.00  │▦ │          │
│             └───────────┴──┘                └───────────┴──┘          │
│  Payment Allocations                                                  │
│  ┌──────┬──────────┬─────────────┬──────────────┬──────────────┬──┐  │
│  │Type  │Date      │Payment Ref  │Details       │       Amount │▲ │  │
│  │      │          │             │              │              │  │  │
│  │      │          │             │              │              │  │  │
│  │      │          │             │              │              │  │  │
│  │      │          │             │              │              │▾ │  │
│  └──────┴──────────┴─────────────┴──────────────┴──────────────┴──┘  │
│                                                      ┌──────────┐     │
│                                                      │  Edit    │     │
│                                                      └──────────┘     │
│                                                      ┌──────────┐     │
│                                                      │  Close   │     │
│                                                      └──────────┘     │
└─────────────────────────────────────────────────────────────────────┘
```

Some corrections that you can make in this way have a bigger effect on the underlying records than others. For example, if you try to change the date or the amounts or account codes for a transaction the program may let you do so, but to guard against fraud it will also post a record of what has been changed, and you will be able to see this if you click on **Modules** and then **Financials**: the correction will show up in red.

Task 11

Let's say that the £20 payment entered in petty cash for a train fare should actually have been £15. We could, of course, make adjustments using a journal entry, but here we will use the correction facility.

In the **File** menu, click on **Maintenance > Corrections**

Look down the list of transactions until you find £20 for the train ticket. Double click on that and enter £15 in the net amount. Save the correction.

Now go to **Bank > Petty Cash** (double click) **> Activity**

You will see that the transaction is now only £15 and the petty cash balance has increased by £5. However, there is a memorandum entry in red stating that £20 has been deleted.

MONTH-END PROCEDURES

Running the month-end procedures allows you to:

- Post prepayments
- Post accruals
- Post depreciation
- Clear the turnover figures. This sets your month to date turnover figures to zero on each customer and supplier record window.

You will not have to set up accruals, prepayments or depreciation in your assessment, but it is important to understand that the month-end procedure allows you to produce monthly accounts, perhaps for comparison with a budget.

The month-end is also a convenient time at which to run the audit trail report (**Modules > Financials > Audit**) which will print out all transactions, and then to clear the audit trail (by selecting **Tools > Period End > Clear Audit Trail**). Clearing the audit trail means that less information has to be held by the system (both live data and back-up data) so that it will operate more efficiently.

To run month-end choose **Company > Manage Month End** (from the task list). This will start up a wizard which guides you through three phases:

Preparation

Post all transactions for the period including recurring entries, set up any pre-payments and/or accruals required, take full account of depreciation in your Fixed Assets Register, optionally reconcile all bank accounts to your bank account statements.

Run month-end

In this phase you create a backup, change your program date to the month-end date, then run the month-end operation to post prepayments, accruals and depreciation, and clear your turnover figures.

Completion

In this third phase you create another backup, then, again optionally, clear your Audit Trail, after which you create another backup.

Starting over

All of us have a bad day sometimes! Occasionally, you may find that you or someone else using the package has made a number of mistakes, perhaps due to a misunderstanding.

If this happens it may well be better to start again rather than trying to correct all the mistakes, possibly making things worse.

To do so, of course, you need to have made a backup of the data as it was before all the errors were made. You can then simply restore the correct data and start posting your new entries again.

This is one of the many advantages of taking regular back-ups!

CHAPTER OVERVIEW

- Payments and receipts should be allocated to outstanding invoices as it is important to know which invoices have been paid

- Bank reconciliations are very important controls in accounting systems and are easily accomplished in Sage

- All the printouts that you are likely to require are available as pre-prepared reports

- There are various facilities for error correction, but it is best not to make errors in the first place!

Keywords

Customer – a person or organisation that buys products or services from your organisation

Customer ledger – the collection of customer accounts, also known as the debtors ledger or sales ledger

Customer record – the details relating to the customer account, for example name and address, contact details and credit terms

Supplier – a person or organisation that your organisation buys products or services from

Suppliers ledger – the collection of supplier accounts, also known as the creditors ledger or purchases ledger

Supplier record – the details relating to the supplier account, for example name and address, contact details and credit terms

TEST YOUR LEARNING

Test 1

When you receive a payment from an account customer this is posted from the Bank menu using the Bank Receipts button. True or False? Explain your answer.

Test 2

Once an entry has been made in Sage, the only way to correct it is to use a journal. True or False?

Test 3

The error correction facility wipes out all trace of the original entry. True or False? Explain you answer.

Test 4

Give one reason why the month-end procedure calculates and clears the monthly expense account balances?

Test 5

Transfers between bank accounts should always be processed by using the Journal facility. True or False?

Test 6

Taking regular back-ups are unnecessary because computerised accounting packages and modern computer equipment are so reliable. True or False?

ANSWERS TO CHAPTER TASKS

CHAPTER 1 Sage – Part 1

Task 1

This is a hands-on activity. You need to start either with a new installation of Sage, or a blank company.

Task 2

This is a hands-on activity. The Name should be Publicity material, the Type is Overheads, the Category is Printing and Stationery. Sage will suggest a Ref (account number) such as 7504 or 7506, and you should accept this. There is no opening balance to enter.

Task 3

Vimal could easily forget to give the account a proper name next time he uses the package and in future he may not have any idea what sort of expense should be recorded in that account. Nobody else who uses the system will have a clue either. The moral of the story is don't use abbreviations that others might not understand, and take care with spelling too. A bit of care will save time in the long run.

Task 4

It is possible for a customer and a supplier to have the same code, because it is quite possible that a business will both sell and buy goods from the same person. Although the accounts would use the same code, the accounts would be held in different ledgers.

Task 5

This is a hands-on activity. One way to complete the task is to use the new supplier wizard and fill in as much detail as possible. When you have finished open your record (make sure that terms are agreed, if necessary) and check the details on screen against those given. The illustration in the Task shows the code MCA001 (consistent with the alpha numeric format recommended earlier in the chapter).

Task 6

This is a hands-on activity.

Task 7

This is a hands-on activity. Make sure that your journal has an appropriate reference and that each line has a description (use the F6 key for the second two lines). You can check your journal by clicking the Financials button, or by looking at the Activity tab of the nominal ledger accounts affected, if you wish.

Task 8

This is a hands-on activity. An example file name would be SFE_A08.XYZ, where A08 stands for Activity 8 and XYZ are your initials, but be sure to ask your lecturer or manager about the file name you should use. If you save the backup to a memory stick, keep it safe and put a label on it. It is evidence of your competence!

Task 9

This is a hands-on activity. Use the F6 key when entering the second line of the invoice, to save typing. The total VAT is £5.74 (£4.07 on the first item, which was given **net**, and £1.67 on the second, where we told you the **gross** amount). Don't forget that you can use the F9 button to calculate the net amount.

Task 10

This is a hands-on activity.

Task 11

This is a hands-on activity. You may should have decided to post the different types of sales (one was products, one was a service) to different sales accounts. You should have renamed the standard sales accounts in Sage to suit your particular business.

Task 12

This is a hands-on activity. Check your Final balance to the one shown at the activity.

CHAPTER 2 Sage – Part 2

Task 1

This is a hands-on activity. Be sure to use the Bank ... Supplier Payment option, not Bank ... Bank Payments.

Task 2

This is a hands-on activity. Be sure to use the Bank ... Customer Receipt option, not Bank ... Bank Receipts.

Tasks 3 to 11

These tasks are all hands-on activities.

TEST YOUR LEARNING – ANSWERS

CHAPTER 1 Sage – Part 1

Test 1

A field is a box on screen in which you enter data or select from a list (similar to a spreadsheet cell).

Test 2

A default is the entry that the accounting package knows will normally be made in a particular field, for example today's date or the nominal code that a purchase from a certain supplier would normally be posted to.

Test 3

Accounting codes are unambiguous and precise, they can be shorter to enter than the account name and they can determine the class of transaction eg 1000 – 1999 = income, 2000 – 2999 = expenses and so on.

Test 4

It is probably not essential to save your work because all your entries are saved as you go along. It is essential to back-up your work, however, because the program may become damaged or you may make incorrect entries next time you use it.

Test 5

When a back-up is restored all the data currently held in the program is overwritten with the data from the back-up.

Test 6

It will not be possible to change the financial year once any data has been posted to the program. At the year-end it is necessary to go through a special procedure in order to move into the next financial year.

Test 7

Details such as company name and address will appear on any documents generated by the program, such as invoices and statements, and these will be sent to customers, so you will look very foolish if you can't even spell your own organisation's details properly.

Test 8

The chart of accounts is a kind of template setting out the structure of the nominal ledger – which accounts are classed as non-current (fixed) assets, which are current assets, which are current liabilities, which are expenses in the income statement (profit and loss account), and so on.

Test 9

Sales, Purchase, Direct Expenses, Overheads.

Test 10

You must set up an account for the supplier in the purchase ledger before you can post an invoice received from the supplier.

Test 11

You can either set a default nominal ledger account when you set up the supplier account, or you can choose the nominal ledger account at the time that you post the invoice.

Test 12

This is false. The system will not allow you to post a journal that does not balance.

Test 13

Obviously, it is good practice to use the correct date for transactions in any system, but in an accounting package dates govern matters such as receivable (debtor) ageing, monthly reports, and, in particular, the way the VAT liability is calculated.

Test 14

It is usually better to post the invoice lines individually. It is essential to do so if the individual expenses need to be posted to different nominal ledger codes.

CHAPTER 2 Sage – Part 2

Test 1

This is false. Receipts from customers with accounts need to be allocated to outstanding invoices. From the **Bank** menu, these receipts are processed using the **Customer Receipt** button.

Test 2

False. Errors can be corrected using the error correction facility.

Test 3

False. That would be dangerous as fraudulent, untraceable changes could be made under the guise of error correction. A memorandum of the original entry is always recorded.

Test 4

So that the monthly results can be compared with budget.

Test 5

False. The transfer should be processed by selecting **Bank** and then **Bank Transfer** from the task list.

Test 6

False. Modern software and hardware are reliable but they do go wrong (as I'm sure you know). Taking a backup in Sage is quick and simple – one day it will save you!

Test your learning – answers

AAT SAMPLE ASSESSMENT

✍ You are now ready to attempt the AAT sample assessment for Computerised Accounting Software.

✍ This AAT sample assessment provided by the AAT uses a standard rate of VAT of 20%.

✍ Answers are provided at the end of the assessment.

Instructions to candidates

This assessment asks you to input data into a computerised accounting package and produce documents and reports. There are 14 tasks and it is important that you attempt all tasks.

The time allowed to complete this Computerised accounting assessment is **2 hours**.

Additional time up to a maximum of 1 hour may be scheduled by your tutor to allow for delays due to computer issues, such as printer queues and uploading documents to LearnPlus.

It is important that you print **all** reports and documents specified in the tasks so your work can be assessed. A checklist has been provided at the end of the assessment to help you check that all documents and reports have been printed. All printed material should be **titled** and marked with your **name** and **AAT membership number**.

If your computerised accounting system allows for the generation of PDFs, these can be generated instead of hard copy prints. Screenshots saved as image files are also acceptable.

If you are using print-outs as evidence, the only document you are required to upload at the end of the assessment is your assessment book. If you have generated PDFs or screenshots instead of printing, these documents should be uploaded to LearnPlus with your assessment book. Your assessor will tell you which option to use.

Data

This assessment is based on an existing business, **Campbell Kitchens**, an organisation that supplies kitchen furniture and equipment. The owner of the business is **Kitty Campbell** who operates as a sole trader.

At the start of business Kitty operated a manual bookkeeping system but has now decided that from **1 May 20XX** the accounting system will become computerised.

You are employed as an accounting technician.

You can assume that all documentation has been checked for accuracy and authorised by Kitty Campbell.

Cash and credit sales are to be analysed in **two** ways:

- Kitchen furniture
- Kitchen equipment

Some nominal ledger accounts have already been allocated account codes. You may need to amend or create other account codes.

The business is registered for VAT. The rate of VAT charged on all goods and services sold by Campbell Kitchens is 20%.

All expenditure should be analysed as you feel appropriate.

Before you start the assessment you should:

- Set the system software date as **31 May of the current year**

- Set the financial year to start on **1 May of the current year**

- Set up the company details by entering the name **Campbell Kitchens** and the address: **47 Landsway Road, Stotton, ST4 9TX**.

This set-up does not form part of the assessment standards, so your training provider may assist you with this.

Task 1

Refer to the **customer listing** below and set up customer records to open sales ledger accounts for each customer, entering opening balances at 1 May 20XX.

Customer Listing

CUSTOMER NAME AND ADDRESS	CUSTOMER ACCOUNT CODE	CUSTOMER ACCOUNT DETAILS AT 1 MAY 20XX
Fraser Designs 291 Tower Way Stotton ST7 4PQ	FRA001	Payment terms: 30 days Opening balance: £2,017.60
Fry and Partners 9 Carters Lane Brigtown BG1 3QT	FRY002	Payment terms: 30 days Opening balance: £1,597.60
SCL Interiors 14 Dingle Street Stotton ST4 2LY	SCL001	Payment terms: 30 days Opening balance: £1,906.50

Task 2

Refer to the **supplier listing** below and set up supplier records to open purchases ledger accounts for each supplier, entering opening balances at 1 May 20XX.

Supplier Listing

SUPPLIER NAME AND ADDRESS	SUPPLIER ACCOUNT CODE	SUPPLIER ACCOUNT DETAILS AT 1 MAY 20XX
Hart Ltd 3 Lion Street Stotton ST8 2HX	HAR001	Payment terms: 30 days Opening balance: £1,012.75
Jackson Builders 75 Stevens Street Brigtown BG5 3PE	JAC001	Payment terms: 30 days Opening balance: £456.35
Vanstone plc 404 Larchway Estate Brigtown BG9 7HJ	VAN001	Payment terms: 30 days Opening balance: £2,097.40

Task 3

Refer to the list of **nominal ledger accounts** below:

(a) Set up nominal ledger records for each account, entering opening balances at 1 May 20XX and making sure you select, amend or create appropriate nominal ledger account codes.

(b) Generate a trial balance, check the accuracy of the trial balance and, if necessary, correct any errors. **You do not need to print the trial balance.**

List of general ledger balances as at 01.05.20XX

ACCOUNT NAMES	Debit balance £	Credit balance £
Motor Vehicles	20,067.10	
Bank current account	4,916.26	
Petty Cash	68.24	
VAT on sales		1,497.68
VAT on purchases	909.23	
Capital		26,416.85
Drawings	350.00	
Sales – kitchen furniture		456.20
Sales – kitchen equipment		119.30
Goods for re-sale	224.00	
Sales ledger control* (see note below)	5,521.70	
Purchases ledger control* (see note below)		3,566.50

* Note:

As you have already entered opening balances for customers and suppliers the software package you are using may not require you to enter these balances.

Task 4

Refer to the following summary of sales invoices and summary of sales credit notes and enter these transactions into the computer.

Summary of sales invoices

Date 20XX	Customer name	Invoice number	Gross £	VAT £	Net £	Kitchen furniture £	Kitchen equipme... £
7 May	Fry and Partners	523	2,011.68	335.28	1,676.40	1,676.40	
21 May	Fraser Designs	524	852.24	142.04	710.20		710.20
	Totals		2,863.92	477.32	2,386.60	1,676.40	710.20

Summary of sales credit notes

Date 20XX	Customer name	Credit note number	Gross £	VAT £	Net £	Kitchen furniture £	Kitchen equipme... £
14 May	Fry and Partners	61	500.16	83.36	416.80	416.80	
	Totals		500.16	83.36	416.80	416.80	0.00

Task 5

Refer to the following purchases invoices and the purchases credit note and enter these transactions into the computer.

Purchases invoices

Jackson Builders
75 Steven Street, Brigtown, BG5 3PE
VAT Registration No 321 3726 89

I N V O I C E   N O 5/219

Date: 12 May 20XX

Campbell Kitchens
47 Landsway Road
Stotton
ST4 9TX

	£
Repairs to building	909.25
VAT @ 20%	181.85
Total for payment	1,091.10

Terms: 30 days

Vanstone plc
404 Larchway Estate, Brigtown, BG9 7HJ
VAT Registration No 119 0799 52

I N V O I C E   N O 2017

Date: 18 May 20XX

Campbell Kitchens
47 Landsway Road
Stotton
ST4 9TX

	£
Supplying goods for re-sale	2,146.80
VAT @ 20%	429.36
Total for payment	2,576.16

Terms: 30 days

Purchases credit note

Vanstone plc
404 Larchway Estate, Brigtown, BG9 7HJ
VAT Registration No 119 0799 52

CREDIT NOTE N O 426

Date: 20 May 20XX

Campbell Kitchens
47 Landsway Road
Stotton
ST4 9TX

	£
Return of goods supplied for re-sale	612.75
VAT @ 20%	122.55
Total for payment	735.30

Terms: 30 days

Task 6

Refer to the following BACS remittance advice notes received from customers and enter these transactions into the computer, making sure you allocate all amounts as shown on each remittance advice note.

SCL Interiors
BACS Remittance Advice

To: Campbell Kitchens   15 May 20XX

An amount of £1,906.50 has been paid directly into your bank account in payment of the balance outstanding at 1 May.

Fry and Partners
BACS Remittance Advice

To: Campbell Kitchens   25 May 20XX

An amount of £1,097.44 has been paid directly into your bank account in payment of the balance outstanding at 1 May and including credit note 61.

Task 7

(a) Refer to the following summary of payments made to suppliers and enter these transactions into the computer, making sure you print a remittance advice as shown in (b) **and** allocate all amounts correctly as shown in the details column.

(b) **Print** a remittance advice to accompany the payment made to Hart Ltd.

Cheques paid listing

Date 20XX	Cheque number	Supplier	£	Details
12 May	006723	Vanstone plc	1,200.00	Payment on account
24 May	006724	Hart Ltd	1,012.75	Payment of opening balance

Task 8

(a) Refer to the following email from Kitty Campbell and enter this transaction into the computer.

Email	
From:	Kitty Campbell
To:	Accounting Technician
Date:	10 May 20XX
Subject:	Premises insurance

Hello

I have today paid our annual premises insurance of £819.40 by business debit card.

Please record this transaction. VAT is not applicable.

Thanks,
Kitty

(b) Refer to the following cash sales listing and enter this transaction into the computer.

Date	Payment method	Details	Amount
24 May 20XX	Cheque	JL Green – kitchen equipment	£474.00 including VAT

Task 9

Refer to the following standing order schedule:

(a) Set up a recurring entry as shown in the standing order schedule below.

(b) **Print** a screen shot of the screen setting up the recurring entry.

(c) Process the first payment.

Details	Amount	Frequency of payment	Total no. of payments	Payment start date 20XX	Payment finish date 20XX
Rent – VAT N/A	£750	One payment every 2 months	3	2 May	2 September

Task 10

(a) Refer to the following petty cash re-imbursement slip and enter this transaction into the computer.

Petty Cash Reimbursement PCR No 29	
Date: 1 May 20XX Cash from the bank account to restore the petty cash account to £150.00.	£81.76

(b) Refer to the following petty cash vouchers and enter these transactions into the computer.

Petty Cash Voucher	
Date 7 May 20XX	**No** PC212
Printer paper – including VAT Receipt attached	£ 45.60

Petty Cash Voucher	
Date 18 May 20XX	**No** PC213
Rail fare	£ 37.90
VAT not applicable	
Receipt attached	

Task 11

Refer to the following journal entries and enter them into the computer.

JOURNAL ENTRIES - 24 May 20XX	£	£
Premises insurance	10.00	
Bank		10.00
Being an error in the amount shown on Kitty Campbell's email of 10 May for premises insurance		

JOURNAL ENTRIES - 24 May 20XX	£	£
Drawings	600.00	
Bank		600.00
Being cash withdrawn from the bank by Kitty Campbell for personal use		

Task 12

Refer to the following bank statement:

(a) Enter the bank interest received (no VAT) which has not yet been accounted for.

(b) Reconcile the bank statement. If the bank statement does not reconcile check your work and make the necessary corrections. **You do not need to print a bank reconciliation statement.**

Rowley Bank plc
505 High Street
Stotton
ST1 9VG

Campbell Kitchens
47 Landsway Road
Stotton
ST4 9TX

Account number 62082176   31 May 20XX

STATEMENT OF ACCOUNT

Date 20XX	Details	Paid out £	Paid in £	Balance £
01 May	Opening balance			4,916.26C
01 May	Cash	81.76		4,834.50C
02 May	James Holdings Ltd – Rent	750.00		4,084.50C
10 May	FH Insurance plc	829.40		3,255.10C
12 May	Cheque 006723	1,200.00		2,055.10C
15 May	BACS – SCL Interiors		1,906.50	3,961.60C
24 May	Cash withdrawn	600.00		3,361.60C
25 May	BACS – Fry and Partners		1,097.44	4,459.04C
28 May	Bank interest received		24.20	4,483.24C
	D = Debit C = Credit			

Task 13

(a)   Select the appropriate option to enter or change a password to protect your accounting data, and **print** a screenshot of the screen which shows clearly where the password would be entered. **You should not enter a password into the computer.**

(b)   Using a file name made up of your name followed by 'CKbackup', back up your work to a suitable storage medium. **Print** a screenshot of the backup screen showing the file name and location of back up data. If, for example, your name is Helen Smith you should use the file name 'HelenSmithCKbackup'. Your assessor will tell you what storage medium you should use.

Task 14

Print the following reports:

- The purchases day book (supplier invoices)
- An aged trade payables analysis
- All sales ledger accounts (customer accounts), showing all transactions within each account
- A trial balance at 31 May 20XX
- The sales ledger control account in the nominal ledger, showing all transactions within the account
- An audit trail, showing full details of all transactions, including details of receipts/payments allocated to items in customer/supplier accounts and details of items in the bank account that have been reconciled

Please note the accounting package you are using may not use exactly the same report names as those shown above, so some alternative names are shown in brackets.

Before you finish your work use the checklist that follows to make sure you have printed all documents and reports as specified in the assessment.

Checklist

Documents and reports	Task	✓ when printed
Remittance advice	7	☐
Screenshot of the recurring entry set up screen	9	☐
Screenshot showing where the password would be entered	13	☐
Screenshot showing the file name and location of backup data	13	☐
Purchases day book (supplier invoices)	14	☐
Aged trade payables analysis	14	☐
Sales ledger accounts (customer accounts), showing all transactions within each account	14	☐
Trial balance at 31 May 20XX	14	☐
Sales ledger control account in the nominal ledger, showing all transactions within the account	14	☐
Audit trail, showing full details of all transactions, including details of receipts/payments allocated to items in customer/supplier accounts and details of items in the bank account that have been reconciled	14	☐

AAT sample assessment – answers

Some answers are given below, although these are not exhaustive. The answers provided are indicative of relevant content within the audit trail, the exact format of which will differ according to the computerised accounting package used.

Task	Transaction type	Account(s)		Date 20XX	Net Amount £	VAT £	Allocated against receipt/ payment ✓	Reconciled with bank statement ✓
1	Customer O/bal	FRA001		01 May	2,017.60			
	Customer O/bal	FRY002		01 May	1,597.60		✓	
	Customer O/bal	SCL001		01 May	1,906.50		✓	
2	Supplier O/bal	HAR001		01 May	1,012.75		✓	
	Supplier O/bal	JAC001		01 May	456.35			
	Supplier O/bal	VAN001		01 May	2,097.40			
3	Dr	Motor vehicles		01 May	20,067.10			
	Dr	Bank current account		01 May	4,916.26			✓
	Dr	Petty cash		01 May	68.24			
	Cr	VAT on sales		01 May	1,497.68			
	Dr	VAT on purchases		01 May	909.23			
	Cr	Capital		01 May	26,416.85			
	Dr	Drawings		01 May	350.00			
	Cr	Sales – kitchen furniture		01 May	456.20			
	Cr	Sales – kitchen equipment		01 May	119.30			
	Dr	Goods for re-sale		01 May	224.00			
	Dr	Sales ledger control*		01 May	5,521.70			
	Cr	Purchases ledger control*		01 May	3,566.50			
		*If appropriate						
4	Sales inv	FRY002	Sales – Kitchen furniture	07 May	1,676.40	335.28		
	Sales inv	FRA001	Sales – Kitchen equip	21 May	710.20	142.04		
	Sales CN	FRY002	Sales – Kitchen furniture	14 May	416.80	83.36	✓	
5	Purchases inv	JAC001	Repairs	12 May	909.25	181.85		
	Purchases inv	VAN001	Goods	18 May	2,146.80	429.36		
	Purchases CN	VAN001	Goods	20 May	612.75	122.55		

Task	Transaction type	Account(s)		Date 20XX	Net Amount £	VAT £	Allocated against receipt/ payment ✓	Reconciled with bank statement ✓
6	Customer receipt	SCL001	Bank	15 May	1,906.50			✓
	Customer receipt	FRY002	Bank	25 May	1,097.44			✓
7	Supplier payment on a/c	VAN001	Bank	12 May	1,200.00			✓
	Supplier payment	HAR001	Bank	24 May	1,012.75			
8	Bank payment	Bank	Premises insurance	10 May	819.40			✓
	Bank receipt	Bank	Sales – Kitchen equip	24 May	395.00	79.00		
9	Bank payment	Bank	Rent – SO/DD	02 May	750.00			✓
10	Dr	Petty cash		01 May	81.76			
	Cr	Bank		01 May	81.76			✓
	Cash payment	Petty cash	Stationery	07 May	38.00	7.60		
	Cash payment	Petty cash	Travel	18 May	37.90			
11	Journal debit	Insurance		24 May	10.00			
	Journal credit	Bank		24 May	10.00			✓
	Journal debit	Drawings		24 May	600.00			
	Journal credit	Bank		24 May	600.00			✓
12	Bank receipt	Bank	Bank interest received	28 May	24.20			✓

Additional guidance for individual tasks

If you struggled with the assessment, we suggest you read the guidance below and attempt the assessment again.

Task 1 (guidance)

All customers listed should be set up. Be careful to set them up as customers rather than suppliers. Enter the dates and opening balances carefully as you will lose marks for inaccuracies. In Sage, when you enter the opening balances for customers this creates a **debit to the sales ledger account** and a **credit to a suspense account**. When you enter either a debit or credit in each of Tasks 1 to 3 using the opening balance options within Sage, the opposite side of the entry will be posted to a suspense account. However as the debits and credits you are given in the assessment are equal, the debits and credits to the suspense account will cancel each other off to a nil value, **if you have entered all opening balances correctly.** If you are left with a suspense account balance, then you will have made a mistake while entering the balances.

Task 2 (guidance)

It is important that you set up all **suppliers** listed and that you set them up as suppliers rather than customers. Enter the dates and opening balances carefully and check that all of your entries match the information you have been given.

Task 3 (guidance)

Be careful when entering the balances and selecting the appropriate nominal accounts to make entries to.

When you have finished entering the data, check you have not missed any accounts by previewing a trial balance. Remember – if you have a suspense account then you have entered something incorrectly.

Task 4 (guidance)

Both invoices and the credit note in the listings need to be entered carefully, ensuring you don't enter the credit note as an invoice as you will be in the habit of posting invoices by the time you get to it. It is very important to select the correct nominal account if you want to score well in this task. Always check you have entered **all** of the transactions.

Task 5 (guidance)

When posting purchase invoices/credit notes make sure you select the right supplier and an appropriate nominal account. Make sure you have accounted for the VAT properly too. Always check you have entered **all** of the transactions.

Tasks 6 and 7 (guidance)

You should use the **Customer Receipt** and **Supplier Payment** buttons when entering customer receipts or supplier payments using Sage, Don't miss out any transactions.

Earlier in this Workbook we covered how to print a remittance advice (see chapter 2). Refer back to this if you struggled with the part of Task 7 that required you to do this.

Task 8 (guidance)

This task requires you to process payments and receipts that are not related to credit transactions with customers or suppliers.

Be careful to note which do have VAT implications and which do not. If the amount already includes VAT you must enter this as the gross amount rather than the net amount.

As always the choice of nominal account is important.

Task 9 (guidance)

Note that you are required to take a screen print in this task and you can do this by pressing **Print Screen** or **PrtScn (or PrtSc)**.

Recurring payments are a bit tricky in Sage as when you first enter the details they do not impact on the nominal ledger. When you go back into Recurring items in Sage to process the payment, remember **you only need to process the first payment.** Details on how to do this were covered in Chapter 2 of this Workbook.

Task 10 (guidance)

In this task you must remember to change the nominal code in Sage to the Petty Cash nominal code when entering the payments in this task.

You can use the **Bank Transfer** button in Sage for the payment from the Bank account to the Petty cash account.

Task 11 (guidance)

Enter journals carefully to ensure you debit and credit the correct accounts. Don't get the debits and credits mixed up.

Task 12 (guidance)

Having entered the bank interest received, you should reconcile the bank using the method covered in Chapter 2. In the answer provided, you can see which items you should have reconciled as they have a tick in the 'Reconciled with bank statement' column.

Task 13 (guidance)

A screenshot is required for **both (a) and (b)**.

In (a) it should clearly show where a password would be entered. In (b) you must make sure you evidence the location of the backup and the file name.

If your screenshots don't clearly evidence all of the above, do them again.

Task 14 (guidance)

This task tests your ability to generate the reports specified. You will get the marks available for this particular task by **generating the correct report**. You will receive these marks even if some of the transactions within the report are incorrect because you entered them incorrectly in earlier tasks.

There is a comprehensive section on generating reports in Chapter 2 of this Workbook. You should look back at this if you were unable to generate and print (hard copy or PDF as appropriate) any reports. **Make sure you check that you have printed all the reports.**

BPP PRACTICE ASSESSMENT

✏ You are now ready to attempt the BPP practice assessment for Computerised Accounting.

✏ This practice assessment uses a standard rate of VAT of 20%.

✏ It requires you to input data into a computerised accounting package and produce documents and reports.

✏ Answers are provided at the end of the assessment.

Instructions to candidates

This assessment asks you to input data into a computerised accounting package and produce documents and reports. There are 14 tasks and it is important that you attempt all tasks.

The time allowed to complete this Computerised Accounting assessment is **2 hours**.

It is important that you print **all** reports and documents specified in the tasks so your work can be assessed. All printed material should be **titled** and marked with your **name** and **membership number**.

If the computerised accounting system allows for the generation of PDFs, these can be generated instead of hard copy prints. Screenshots saved as image files are also acceptable.

Data

This assessment is based on an existing business, Steadman Computer Solutions (SCS), an organisation that supplies computers to local businesses. It also offers a computer repair service. The owner of the business is James Steadman who operates as a sole trader.

James is changing from a manual book-keeping system to a computerised one from 1 January 20XX. You are employed as an accounting technician.

You can assume that all documentation has been checked for accuracy and authorised by James Steadman.

Sales are to be analysed in three ways:

- Desktop computers
- Laptop computers
- Computer repairs

Some general ledger accounts have already been allocated account codes. You may need to amend or create other account codes.

The business is registered for VAT. The rate of VAT charged on all goods and services sold by SCS is 20%.

All expenditure should be analysed as you feel appropriate.

Before you start the assessment you should:

- Set the system software date as **31st January of the current year**.

- Set up the company (in this case a sole trader business) details under the name 'Steadman Computer Solutions'.

- Set the financial year to start on **1st January of the current year**.

This set-up does not form part of the assessment standards, so your training provider may assist you with this.

Task 1

Refer to the customer listing below and set up customer records to open sales ledger accounts for each customer, entering opening balances at 1 January 20XX.

Customer Listing

CUSTOMER NAME, ADDRESS AND CONTACT DETAILS	CUSTOMER ACCOUNT CODE	CUSTOMER ACCOUNT DETAILS AT 1 JANUARY 20XX
Always Insurance plc 26 High Road Cheltenham GL52 8KK Telephone: 01242 276 4366	ALW01	Credit limit: £7,000 Payment terms: 30 days Opening balance: £1,821.70
Local Bank Ltd 56 Long Lane Gloucester GL10 8BN Telephone: 01452 498 222	LOC01	Credit limit: £6,000 Payment terms: 30 days Opening balance: £1,300.00
Large Firm LLP 1 Main Road Swindon SN3 1PP Telephone: 01793 858 349	LAR01	Credit limit: £4,000 Payment terms: 30 days Opening balance: £800.80

Task 2

Refer to the supplier listing below and set up supplier records to open purchases ledger accounts for each supplier, entering opening balances at 1 January 20XX.

Supplier Listing

SUPPLIER NAME, ADDRESS AND CONTACT DETAILS	SUPPLIER ACCOUNT CODE	SUPPLIER ACCOUNT DETAILS AT 1 JANUARY 20XX
Bell Computers Ltd 15 Queen Street London W12 9ZZ Telephone: 0208 740 1020	BEL01	Credit limit: £6,000 Payment terms: 30 days Opening balance: £1,400.00
Discount IT Supplies 50 Banner Place Gloucester GL10 4GG Telephone: 01452 456 983	DIS01	Credit limit: £3,500 Payment terms: 30 days Opening balance: £790.40
Anderson Garages 19 Anderson Road Cheltenham GL51 5JR Telephone: 01242 897 991	AND01	Credit limit: £1,100 Payment terms: 30 days Opening balance: £178.80

Task 3

Refer to the list of general ledger balances below:

- Enter the opening balances into the computer, making sure you select, amend or create appropriate general ledger account codes.

- Check the accuracy of the trial balance and, if necessary, correct any errors.

List of general ledger balances as at 01.01.20XX

ACCOUNT NAMES	£	£
Office Equipment	3,567.00	
Motor Vehicles	12,750.00	
Bank	3101.80	
Petty Cash	200.00	
Sales ledger control* (see note below)	3,922.50	
Purchases ledger control* (see note below)		2,369.20
VAT on sales		1,540.60
VAT on purchases	1,080.20	
Capital		20,000.00
Drawings	4,660.10	
Sales – Desktops		8,780.00
Sales – Laptops		5,920.00
Sales – Computer repairs		620.80
Computers for resale – purchases	8,880.20	
Rent and rates	810.00	
Motor vehicle expenses	258.80	

* Note:
As you have already entered opening balances for customers and suppliers the software package you are using may not require you to enter these balances.

Task 4

Refer to the following sales invoices and sales credit notes and enter these transactions into the computer.

Steadman Computer Solutions
50, George Street, Cheltenham, GL50 1XR
VAT Registration No 478 3164 00

Telephone: 01242 866 5128
Email: J.Steadman@SCS.co.uk

S A L E S   I N V O I C E N O 0100

Date: 01 January 20XX

Local Bank Ltd
56 Long Lane
Gloucester
GL10 8BN

	£
2 new laptops	800.00
VAT @ 20%	160.00
Total for payment	960.00

Terms: 30 days

Steadman Computer Solutions
50, George Street, Cheltenham, GL50 1XR
VAT Registration No 478 3164 00

Telephone: 01242 866 5128
Email: J.Steadman@SCS.co.uk

SALES INVOICE NO 0101

Date: 15 January 20XX

Large Firm LLP
1 Main Road
Swindon
SN3 1PP

	£
5 new desktop PCs	2,520.50
VAT @ 20%	504.10
Total for payment	3,024.60

Terms: 30 days

Steadman Computer Solutions
50, George Street, Cheltenham, GL50 1XR
VAT Registration No 478 3164 00

Telephone: 01242 866 5128
Email: J.Steadman@SCS.co.uk

SALES CREDIT NOTE NO 0020

Date: 18 January 20XX

Local Bank Ltd
56 Long Lane
Gloucester
GL10 8BN

	£
Return of unwanted laptop	400.00
VAT @ 20%	80.00
Total for payment	480.00

Terms: 30 days

Steadman Computer Solutions
50, George Street, Cheltenham, GL50 1XR
VAT Registration No 478 3164 00

Telephone: 01242 866 5128
Email: J.Steadman@SCS.co.uk

S A L E S   I N V O I C E   N O   0102

Date: 25 January 20XX

Always Insurance plc
26 High Road
Cheltenham

GL52 8KK

	£
10 laptops	3,950.00
VAT @ 20%	790.00
Total for payment	4,740.00

Terms: 30 days

Task 5

Refer to the following summary of purchase invoices and enter these transactions into the computer.

Summary of purchase invoices

Date 20XX	Supplier Name	Invoice Number	Gross £	VAT £	Net £	Computers for resale £	Motor expenses £
03.01.XX	Bell Computers	SC2040	2,520.00	420.00	2,100.00	2,100.00	
09.01.XX	Anderson Garages	R2168	192.00	32.00	160.00		160.00
21.01.XX	Discount IT Supplies	1806	2,493.60	415.60	2,078.00	2,078.00	
	Totals		5,205.60	867.60	4,338.00	4,178.00	160.00

Task 6

(a) Refer to the following summary of payments received from customers and enter these transactions into the computer, making sure you allocate all amounts as shown in the details column.

Cheque/BACS receipts listing

Date	Receipt type	Customer	£	Details
14.01.XX	BACS	Always Insurance plc	1,821.70	Payment of opening balance
26.01.XX	Cheque	Local Bank Ltd	480.00	Payment of invoice 0100 including credit note 0020

(b) Print a customer statement for Local Bank Ltd at 31 January 20XX.

Task 7

Refer to the following summary of payments made to suppliers and enter these transactions into the computer, making sure you allocate all amounts as shown in the details column.

Cheques paid listing

Date	Cheque number	Supplier	£	Details
11.01.XX	003241	Bell Computers Ltd	1,000.00	Payment on account
20.01.XX	003242	Anderson Garages	192.00	Payment of invoice R2168
23.01.XX	003243	Discount IT Supplies	790.40	Payment of opening balance

Task 8

(a) Refer to the following receipt issued for cash sales and enter this transaction into the computer.

Receipt Number 06
Date   07 January 20XX
Received, by cheque, for a minor repair to a laptop computer: £60.00 including VAT

(b) Refer to the following email below from James Steadman and enter this transaction into the computer.

Email
From: James Steadman **To:**   Accounting Technician **Date:**   12 January 20XX **Subject:**   Drawings
Hello I have withdrawn £180 in cash from the business bank for my personal use. Please record this transaction. Thanks James

(c) Refer to the following cash purchases listing and enter this transaction into the computer.

Date	Payment method	Details	Amount
23 January 20XX	Debit card	Purchase of James Steadman's business laptop computer	£450.00 including VAT

Task 9

Refer to the following direct debit details:

(a)   Set up a recurring entry as shown in the table below.

(b)   **Print** a screen shot of the screen setting up the recurring entry.

(c)   Process the first payment.

Direct debit details

Details	Amount	First payment	Number of monthly payments
Rates	£300	24 January 20XX	12

Task 10

(a)   Refer to the following petty cash vouchers and enter the petty cash payments into the computer.

Petty Cash Voucher	
Date 16 January 20XX	**No** PC042
Train ticket for business travel – VAT not applicable Receipt attached	£ 38.00

Petty Cash Voucher	
Date 20 January 20XX	**No** PC043
A4 pads, folders and ball point pens VAT Total Receipt attached	£ 31.60 6.32 37.92

(b)   Refer to the following petty cash re-imbursement slip and enter this transaction into the computer.

Petty Cash Reimbursement PCR No 03	
Date: 31 January 20XX Cash from the bank account to restore the petty cash account to £200.00.	£75.92

Task 11

Refer to the following journal entries and enter them into the computer.

JOURNAL ENTRIES TO BE MADE 15.01.XX	£	£
Drawings	85.00	
Motor expenses		85.00

Being journal to reflect personal motor expenses posted as business expenses

JOURNAL ENTRIES TO BE MADE 30.01.XX	£	£
Sales - Desktops	400.00	
Sales - Laptops		400.00

Being correction of an error in where a Laptop sale was originally incorrectly recorded as a Desktop sale

Task 12

Refer to the following bank statement:

- Enter the bank charges paid not yet accounted for.

- Reconcile the bank statement. If the bank statement does not reconcile check your work and make the necessary corrections.

<table>
<tr><td colspan="5">South Bank plc
60 Broad Street
Cheltenham
GL51 9YY</td></tr>
<tr><td colspan="5">Steadman Computer Solutions
50 Broad Street
Cheltenham
GL50 1XR
Account number 00698435

31 January 20XX</td></tr>
<tr><td colspan="5" align="center">STATEMENT OF ACCOUNT</td></tr>
<tr><td>Date
20XX</td><td>Details</td><td>Paid out
£</td><td>Paid in
£</td><td>Balance
£</td></tr>
<tr><td>01 Jan</td><td>Opening balance</td><td></td><td></td><td>3,101.80C</td></tr>
<tr><td>09 Jan</td><td>Counter credit</td><td></td><td>60.00</td><td>3,161.80C</td></tr>
<tr><td>12 Jan</td><td>Cash withdrawal</td><td>180.00</td><td></td><td>2,981.80C</td></tr>
<tr><td>14 Jan</td><td>BACS: Always Insurance plc</td><td></td><td>1,821.70</td><td>4,803.50C</td></tr>
<tr><td>14 Jan</td><td>Cheque 003241</td><td>1000.00</td><td></td><td>3,803.50C</td></tr>
<tr><td>23 Jan</td><td>Debit card</td><td>450.00</td><td></td><td>3,353.50C</td></tr>
<tr><td>24 Jan</td><td>Cheque 003242</td><td>192.00</td><td></td><td>3,161.50C</td></tr>
<tr><td>24 Jan</td><td>Direct Debit – Cheltenham MBC – Rates</td><td>300.00</td><td></td><td>2,861.50C</td></tr>
<tr><td>28 Jan</td><td>Deposit</td><td></td><td>480.00</td><td>3,341.50C</td></tr>
<tr><td>29 Jan</td><td>Cheque 003243</td><td>790.40</td><td></td><td>2,551.10C</td></tr>
<tr><td>30 Jan</td><td>Bank charges</td><td>12.40</td><td></td><td>2,538.70C</td></tr>
<tr><td>31 Jan</td><td>Transfer</td><td>75.92</td><td></td><td>2,462.78C</td></tr>
<tr><td></td><td>D = Debit   C = Credit</td><td></td><td></td><td></td></tr>
</table>

Task 13

(a) Use the password 'CPAGm3' to protect your accounting data and **print** a screenshot of the screen showing the entry of the password into the computer.

(b)   Use a file name made up of your name followed by 'SCSbackup' and back up your work to a suitable storage medium. **Print** a screenshot of the backup screen showing the file name and location of back up data. If, for example, your name is Jack Jones you should use the file name 'JackJonesSCSbackup'. Your assessor will tell you what storage medium you should use.

Task 14

(a)   Print a trial balance as at 31 January 20XX. Check the accuracy of the trial balance and, if necessary, correct any errors.

(b)   Print the following reports.

- The sales day book (customer invoices)

- The sales returns day book (customer credits)

- The purchases day book (supplier invoices)

- An aged trade receivables analysis

- All sales ledger accounts (customer accounts), showing all transactions within each account

- All purchases ledger accounts (supplier accounts), showing all transactions within each account

- A trial balance at 31 January 2013

- An audit trail, showing full details of all transactions, including details of receipts/payments allocated to items in customer/supplier accounts and details of items in the bank account that have been reconciled.

Please note the accounting package you are using may not use exactly the same report names as those shown above, so some alternative names are shown in brackets.

BPP practice assessment – answers

Some answers are given below. The answers we've provided are indicative of relevant content within the audit trail, the exact format of which will differ according to the computerised accounting package used.

Task	Transaction type	Account(s)		Date 20XX	Net Amount £	VAT £	Allocated against receipt/ payment ✓	Reconciled with bank statement ✓
1	Customer O/bal	ALW01		01 Jan	1,821.70		✓	
	Customer O/bal	LOC01		01 Jan	1,300.00			
	Customer O/bal	LAR01		01 Jan	800.80			
2	Supplier O/bal	BEL01		01 Jan	1,400.00			
	Supplier O/bal	DIS01		01 Jan	790.40		✓	
	Supplier O/bal	AND01		01 Jan	178.80			
3	Dr	Office equipment		01 Jan	3,567.00			
	Dr	Motor vehicles		01 Jan	12,750.00			
	Dr	Bank current account		01 Jan	3,101.80			✓
	Dr	Petty cash		01 Jan	200.00			
	Dr	Sales ledger control		01 Jan	3,922.50			
	Cr	Purchases ledger control		01 Jan	2,369.20			
	Cr	VAT on sales		01 Jan	1,540.60			
	Dr	VAT on purchases		01 Jan	1,080.20			
	Cr	Capital		01 Jan	20,000.00			
	Dr	Drawings		01 Jan	4,660.10			
	Cr	Sales – Desktops		01 Jan	8,780,00			
	Cr	Sales – Laptops		01 Jan	5,920.00			
	Cr	Sales – Computer repairs		01 Jan	620.80			
	Dr	Computers for re-sale – purchases		01 Jan	8,880.20			
	Dr	Rent and rates		01 Jan	810.00			
	Dr	Motor vehicle expenses		01 Jan	258.80			
4	Sales inv	LOC01	Sales – Laptops	01 Jan	800.00	160.00	✓	
	Sales inv	LAR01	Sales – Desktops	15 Jan	2,520.50	504.10		
	Sales CN	LOC01	Sales – Laptops	18 Jan	400.00	80.00	✓	
	Sales inv	ALW01	Sales – Laptops	25 Jan	3,950.00	790.00		
5	Purchases inv	BEL01	Computers for re-sale	03 Jan	2,100.00	420.00		
	Purchases inv	AND01	Motor vehicle expenses	09 Jan	160.00	32.00	✓	
	Purchases inv	DIS01	Computers for re-sale	21 Jan	2078.00	415.60		

Task	Transaction type	Account(s)		Date 20XX	Net Amount £	VAT £	Allocated against receipt/ payment ✓	Reconciled with bank statement ✓
6	Customer receipt	ALW01	Bank	14 Jan	1,821.70			✓
	Customer receipt	LOC01	Bank	26 Jan	480.00			✓
7	Supplier payment on a/c	BEL01	Bank	11 Jan	1,000.00			✓
	Supplier payment	AND01	Bank	20 Jan	192.00			✓
	Supplier payment	DIS01	Bank	23 Jan	790.40			✓
8	Bank receipt	Bank	Sales – Computer repairs	07 Jan	50.00	10.00		✓
	Bank payment	Bank	Drawings	12 Jan	180.00			✓
	Bank payment	Bank	Office equipment	23 Jan	375.00	75.00		✓
9	Bank payment	Bank	Rates – DD	24 Jan	300.00			✓
10	Cash payment	Petty cash	Travel	16 Jan	38.00			
	Cash payment	Petty cash	Stationery	20 Jan	31.60	6.32		
	Dr	Petty cash		31 Jan	75.92			
	Cr	Bank		31 Jan	75.92			✓
11	Journal debit	Drawings		15 Jan	85.00			
	Journal credit	Motor expenses		15 Jan	85.00			
	Journal debit	Sales – Desktops		30 Jan	400.00			
	Journal credit	Sales – Laptops		30 Jan	400.00			
12	Bank payment	Bank	Bank charges	30 Jan	12.40			✓

Additional guidance for individual tasks

If you struggled with the assessment, we suggest you read the guidance that follows and attempt the assessment again.

Task 1 (guidance)

Make sure you set up all **customers** listed and be careful to set them up as customers rather than suppliers. Enter the dates and opening balances carefully and check that all of your entries match the information you have been given.

Task 2 (guidance)

Make sure you set up all **suppliers** listed and be careful to set them up as suppliers rather than customers. Enter the dates and opening balances carefully and check that all of your entries match the information you have been given.

Task 3 (guidance)

To help reduce the chance of error, be careful and methodical when entering the balances and selecting the appropriate nominal accounts. When finished, check you have not missed any accounts – you can do this by previewing a trial balance. Assuming you entered Task 1 and 2 data correctly, if you are using Sage you will not need to enter opening balances for the sales ledger and purchase ledger control.

Task 4 (guidance)

Enter the invoices and the credit note carefully, ensuring you don't enter the credit note as an invoice or *vice-versa*. Remember that it is very important to select the correct nominal account. You have three sales nominal accounts, and it is clear from the invoices which type of sale each invoice relates to. Always check you have entered **all** of the transactions.

Task 5 (guidance)

When posting purchase invoices make sure you select the right supplier and an appropriate nominal account. VAT should be correctly accounted for and if you set the correct tax code in Sage this will be calculated automatically – all you need to do then is check it matches the VAT shown on the invoice. Always check you have entered **all** of the transactions.

Tasks 6 and 7 (guidance)

When entering customer receipts or supplier payments using Sage you should use the **Customer Receipt** and **Supplier Payment** buttons (not the Bank Receipt/Bank Payment buttons) as demonstrated earlier in this Workbook. You should find this makes it easy to allocate the receipt/payment to the correct customer/supplier account. Don't miss out any transactions.

Earlier in this Workbook we covered how to print a statement for a customer (see Chapter 2). Refer back to this if you struggled with the part of Task 6 that required you to do this.

Task 8 (guidance)

This task requires you to process payments and receipts that are not related to credit transactions with customers or suppliers.

Be careful to note which do have VAT implications and which do not. If the amount already includes VAT you must enter this as the gross amount rather than the net amount.

As always the choice of nominal account is important. Be careful not to omit any payments or receipts.

Task 9 (guidance)

Note that you are required to take a screen print in this task and you can do this by pressing **Print Screen** or **PrtScn (or PrtSc)**.

Recurring payments are a bit tricky in Sage as when you first enter the details they do not impact on the nominal ledger. When you go back into Recurring items in Sage to process the payment, remember **you only need to process the first payment.** Details on how to do this were covered in Chapter 2 of this Workbook.

Task 10 (guidance)

Remember to change the nominal code in Sage to the Petty Cash nominal code when entering the payments in this task.

You can use the **Bank Transfer** button in Sage for the payment from the Bank account to the Petty cash account.

Task 11 (guidance)

Journals should be entered carefully to ensure you debit and credit the correct accounts. Don't get the debits and credits mixed up.

Task 12 (guidance)

Having entered the bank charges, you should reconcile the bank using the method covered in Chapter 2. In the answer provided, you can see which items you should have reconciled as they have a tick in the 'Reconciled with bank statement' column.

Task 13 (guidance)

A screenshot is required for **both (a) and (b)**.

In (a) it should clearly show where a password would be entered. In (b) you must make sure you evidence the location of the backup and the file name.

If your screenshots don't clearly evidence all of the above, do them again.

Task 14 (guidance)

This task tests your ability to generate the reports specified. You will get the marks available for this particular task by **generating the correct report**. You will receive these marks even if some of the transactions within the report are incorrect because you entered them incorrectly in earlier tasks.

There is a comprehensive section on generating reports in Chapter 2 of this Workbook. You should look back at this if you were unable to generate and print (hard copy or PDF as appropriate) any reports. **Make sure you check that you have printed all the reports.**

INDEX

Notes

Notes

Notes

REVIEW FORM

How have you used this Workbook?
(Tick one box only)

☐ Home study

☐ On a course_____

☐ Other _____

Why did you decide to purchase this Workbook? *(Tick one box only)*

☐ Have used BPP Workbooks in the past

☐ Recommendation by friend/colleague

☐ Recommendation by a college lecturer

☐ Saw advertising

☐ Other _____

During the past six months do you recall seeing/receiving either of the following?
(Tick as many boxes as are relevant)

☐ Our advertisement in Accounting Technician

☐ Our Publishing Catalogue

Which (if any) aspects of our advertising do you think are useful?
(Tick as many boxes as are relevant)

☐ Prices and publication dates of new editions

☐ Information on Workbook content

☐ Details of our free online offering

☐ None of the above

Your ratings, comments and suggestions would be appreciated on the following areas of this Workbook.

	Very useful	Useful	Not useful
Introductory section	☐	☐	☐
Quality of explanations	☐	☐	☐
How it works	☐	☐	☐
Chapter tasks	☐	☐	☐
Chapter overviews	☐	☐	☐
Test your learning	☐	☐	☐
Index	☐	☐	☐

	Excellent	Good	Adequate	Poor
Overall opinion of this Workbook	☐	☐	☐	☐

Do you intend to continue using BPP Products?   ☐ Yes   ☐ No

Please note any further comments and suggestions/errors on the reverse of this page or email them to: ianblackmore@bpp.com

Please return to: Ian Blackmore, AAT Range Manager, BPP Learning Media Ltd, FREEPOST, London, W12 8AA.

REVIEW FORM (continued)

TELL US WHAT YOU THINK

Please note any further comments and suggestions/errors below.